卞尺丹几乙し丹卞と
Translated Language Learning

The Country of the Blind
盲人の国
H.G. Wells

English / 日本語

Copyright © 2024 Tranzlaty
All rights reserved.
Published by Tranzlaty
ISBN: 978-1-83566-238-0
Original text by H.G. Wells
The Country of the Blind
First published in English in 1904
www.tranzlaty.com

Three hundred miles and more from Chimborazo
チンボラソから300マイル以上
one hundred miles from the snows of Cotopaxi
コトパクシの雪から100マイル
in the wildest wastes of Ecuador's Andes
エクアドルのアンデス山脈の最も荒々しい荒野で
cut off from all the world of men
人間のすべての世界から切り離された
there lies the mysterious mountain valley
そこには神秘的な山の谷があります
the Country of the Blind
盲人の国
Long years ago, that valley was open to the world
遠い昔、あの渓谷は世界に開かれていた
men came through frightful gorges and over an icy pass
男たちは恐ろしい峡谷を通り抜け、凍った峠を越えてきた
from there they could get into the valley's equable meadows
そこから渓谷の平坦な牧草地に入ることができた
and men did indeed come to the valley this way
そして、人々は確かにこのように谷に来た
some families of Peruvian half-breeds came
ペルーの混血種の家族が何人か来ました
they were fleeing from the tyranny of an evil Spanish ruler
彼らは邪悪なスペインの支配者の圧政から逃れていたのです
Then came the stupendous outbreak of Mindobamba
その後、ミンドバンバの驚異的な発生が起こりました
it was night in Quito for seventeen days
キトの夜は17日間続いた
and the water was boiling at Yaguachi

そして、ヤグアチで水が沸騰していました
the fish were dying as far as Guayaquil
魚はグアヤキルまで死んでいた
everywhere along the Pacific slopes there were land-slips
太平洋の斜面沿いのいたるところに地滑りがありました
and there was swift thawings and sudden floods
そして、急激な雪解けと突然の洪水がありました
one whole side of the old Arauca crest slipped
古いアラウカの紋章の片側全体が滑った
it all came down in a thunderous moment
すべては雷鳴のような瞬間に降り注いだ
this cut off access to the Country of the Blind for ever
これにより、盲人の国へのアクセスが永遠に遮断されました
the exploring feet of men wondered that way no more
探り探りの足は、もはやそのようには思わなかった
But one of these early settlers happened to be close by
しかし、これらの初期の入植者の一人がたまたま近くにいました
he was on the other side of the gorges that day
その日、彼は峡谷の向こう側にいた
the day that the world had so terribly shaken itself
世界がひどく揺れ動いた日
he had to forget his wife and his children
彼は妻と子供たちのことを忘れなければならなかった
and he had to forget all his friends and possessions
そして、彼はすべての友人と所有物を忘れなければなりませんでした
and he had to start life over again
そして、彼は人生をやり直さなければなりませんでした
a new life in the lower world
下界での新しい生活
but illness and blindness took hold of him

しかし、病気と盲目が彼を捕らえました
and he died of punishment in the mines
そして彼は鉱山で罰を受けて死んだ
but the story he told begot a legend
しかし、彼が語った物語は伝説を生んだ
a legend that lingers to this day
今も語り継がれる伝説
and it travels the length of Andes
そしてそれはアンデスの長さを旅します
He told of his reason for venturing back from that fastness
彼は、その潔癖さから立ち直った理由を語った
the place into which he had been carried
彼が運ばれた場所
he had been taken to that place as a child
彼は子供の頃にその場所に連れて行かれました
lashed to a llama, beside a vast bale of gear
ラマに鞭打たれ、巨大な装備の俵のそばに
He said the valley had all that the heart of man could desire
彼は、渓谷には人間の心が望むことができるすべてのものがあると言いました
sweet water, pasture, an even climate
甘い水、牧草地、均一な気候
slopes of rich brown soil and tangles of a shrub
豊かな茶色の土壌と低木のもつれの斜面
he spoke of bushes that bore an excellent fruit
彼は、素晴らしい実を結ぶ茂みについて話しました
on one side there were great hanging forests of pine
片側には松の大きな吊り下げられた森がありました
the pine had held the avalanches high
松は雪崩を高く支えていた
Far overhead, on three sides, there were vast cliffs
遥か頭上には、三方に巨大な崖があった

they were of a grey-green rock
それらは灰緑色の岩でできていた
and at the top there were caps of ice
そして頂上には氷のキャップがありました
but the glacier stream came not to them
しかし、氷河の流れは彼らには来なかった
it flowed away by the farther slopes
それは遠い斜面から流れ去った
and only now and then huge ice masses fell
そして、時折、巨大な氷の塊が落ちてきました
In this valley it neither rained nor snowed
この渓谷では雨も雪も降らなかった
but the abundant springs gave a rich green pasture
しかし、豊富な泉は豊かな緑の牧草地を与えました
their irrigation spread over all the valley space
その灌漑は渓谷全体に広がっていた
The settlers there did well indeed
そこの入植者たちは確かによくやった
Their beasts did well and multiplied
彼らの獣はうまくいき、増殖しました
only one thing marred their happiness
彼らの幸せを損ないだものはただ一つ
And it was enough to mar their happiness greatly
そして、それは彼らの幸福を大きく損なうのに十分でした
A strange disease had come upon them
奇妙な病気が彼らに襲い掛かってきたのだ
it made all their children blind
それは彼らの子供たち全員を盲目にしました
He was sent to find some charm or antidote
彼はおまじないや解毒剤を見つけるために送られました
a cure against this plague of blindness
この盲目の疫病に対する治療法
so he returned down the gorge

それで彼は峡谷を下って戻った
but not without fatigue, danger, and difficulty
しかし、疲労、危険、困難がないわけではありません
In those days men did not think of germs
当時、男性は細菌のことを考えていませんでした
sin explained why this had happened
シンはなぜこのようなことが起こったのかを説明しました
this is what he thought too
彼もそう思った
there was a cause for this affliction
この苦しみには原因がありました
the immigrants had been without a priest
移民は司祭を欠いていた
they had failed to set up a shrine
彼らは神社を建てることに失敗したのです
this should have been the first thing they did
これは彼らが最初にすべきことでした
He wanted to build a shrine
彼は神社を建てたかったのです
a handsome, cheap, effectual shrine
ハンサムで、安く、効果的な神社
he wanted it to be erected in the valley
彼はそれを谷に建てることを望んでいました
he wanted relics and such-like
彼は遺物などを欲しがっていた
he wanted potent things of faith
彼は力強い信仰のものを欲しがった
he wanted blessed objects and mysterious medals
彼は祝福された物と神秘的なメダルを欲しがっていました
and he felt they needed prayers
そして、彼らには祈りが必要だと感じました
In his wallet he had a bar of silver

財布には銀の延べ棒が入っていました
but he would not say from where it was
しかし、彼はそれがどこから来たのかは言わなかった
he insisted there was no silver in the valley
彼は谷に銀はないと主張した
and he had the insistence of an inexpert liar
そして、彼は専門家の嘘つきの主張を持っていました
They had collected their money and ornaments
彼らはお金と装飾品を集めました
he said they had little need for such treasure
彼は、そのような宝物はほとんど必要ないと言いました
he told them he would buy them holy help
彼は彼らに聖なる助けを買うと言いました
even though this was against their will
それが彼らの意思に反していたとしても
he was sunburnt, gaunt, and anxious
彼は日焼けし、やつれ、不安だった
he was unused to the ways of the lower world
彼は下界のやり方に慣れていなかった
clutching his hat feverishly he told his story
帽子を無我夢中で握りしめながら、彼は自分の物語を語った
he told his story to some keen-eyed priest
彼は鋭い目つきの司祭に自分の話をした
he secured some holy remedies
彼はいくつかの聖なる救済策を確保しました
blessed water, statues, crosses and prayer books
祝福された水、彫像、十字架、祈祷書
and he sought to return and save his people
そして、彼は戻ってきて民を救おうとしました
he came to the where the gorge had been
彼は峡谷があったところに来ました
but in front of him was a mass of fallen stone
しかし、目の前には落ちた石の塊があった

imagine his infinite dismay
彼の無限の狼狽を想像してみてください
he had been expelled by nature from his land
彼は自然によって彼の土地から追放されたのです
But the rest of his story of mischances is lost
しかし、彼の不運な物語の残りの部分は失われています
all we know of is his evil death after several years
私たちが知っているのは、数年後の彼の邪悪な死だけです

a poor stray from that remoteness!
あの辺境の地から哀れな迷い！
The stream that had once made the gorge diverted
かつて峡谷を作った小川は迂回していた
now it bursts from the mouth of a rocky cave
今は岩だらけの洞窟の口から飛び出しています
and the legend of his story took on its own life
そして、彼の物語の伝説は、それ自体が命を吹き込まれた
it developed into the legend one may still hear today
それは今日でも聞くことができる伝説に発展しました
a race of blind men "somewhere over there"
盲目の男たちの種族「どこかあそこ」
the little population was now isolated
僅かな人口は今や孤立していた
the valley was forgotten by the outside world
渓谷は外の世界から忘れ去られていた
and their disease ran its course
そして、彼らの病気はその経過をたどりました
The old had to grope to find their way
老人たちは手探りで道を見つけなければならなかった
the young could see a little, but dimly
若者は少し見えたが、ぼんやりと見えた
and the newborns never saw at all
そして、新生児はまったく見えませんでした

But life was very easy in the valley
しかし、渓谷での生活はとても楽でした
there were neither thorns nor briars
棘も茨もなかった
there were no evil insects in the land
この地には邪悪な昆虫はいなかった
and there were no dangerous beasts
そして、危険な獣はいませんでした
a gentle breed of llamas grazed the valley
穏やかなラマの品種が渓谷を放牧していました
those that could see had become purblind gradually
目が見えるものは、次第に盲目になっていった
so their loss was scarcely noticed
そのため、彼らの損失はほとんど気づかれませんでした
The elders guided the sightless youngsters
年長者たちは、目の見えない若者たちを導いた
and the young soon knew the whole valley marvellously
若者はすぐに谷全体をすばらしく知りました
even when the last sight died out, the race lived on
最後の光景が消えても、レースは生き続けた
There had been enough time to adapt
適応するのに十分な時間があった
they learned the control of fire
彼らは火の制御を学んだ
they carefully put it in stoves of stone
彼らはそれを石のストーブに注意深く入れました
at first they were a simple strain of people
最初は、彼らは単純な株の人々でした
they had never had books or writing
彼らは本も書いたこともありませんでした
and they were only slightly touched by Spanish civilisation
そして、彼らはスペイン文明にほんの少しだけ触れまし

た
although they had some of the Peruvian traditions and arts
彼らはペルーの伝統と芸術のいくつかを持っていましたが

and they kept some of those philosophies alive
そして、彼らはそれらの哲学のいくつかを生かし続けました

Generation followed generation
世代に次ぐ世代

They forgot many things from the world
彼らはこの世の多くのことを忘れてしまった

but they also devised many new things
しかし、彼らはまた多くの新しいことを考案しました

the greater world they came from became mythical
彼らがやってきた大いなる世界は神話となった

colours and details were uncertain
色やディテールは不確かでした

and reference to sight became a metaphor
そして、視覚への言及は比喩になりました

In all things apart from sight they were strong and able
視覚以外のすべてのことにおいて、彼らは強く、有能であった

occasionally one with an original mind was born to them
時折、独創的な心を持った者が生まれました

someone who could talk and persuade
話して説得できる人

These passed away, leaving their effects
これらは、その影響を残して亡くなりました

and the little community grew in numbers
そして、小さなコミュニティは数を増やしていきました

and their understanding of their world grew
そして、彼らの世界に対する理解が深まりました

and they settled social and economic problems that arose
そして、彼らは生じた社会的および経済的問題を解決しました
Generations followed more generations
世代はさらに多くの世代に続いた
fifteen generations had passed since that ancestor left
その祖先が去ってから15世代が経っていた
the ancestor who took the bar of silver
銀の延べ棒を取った祖先
the ancestor who went to find God's aid
神の助けを求めに行った祖先
the ancestor who never returned to the valley
渓谷に帰ることのない祖先
but fifteen generations later a new man came
しかし、15世代後、新しい人がやってきました
a man from the outside world
外の世界から来た男
a man who happened to find the valley of the blind
たまたま見つけた盲人の谷
this is the story of that man
これはあの男の物語です
He was a mountaineer from the country near Quito
彼はキト近郊の登山家でした
a man who had been down to the sea
海に沈んでいた男
a man who had seen the world
世界を見た男
a reader of books in an original way
独創的な方法で本を読む
an acute and enterprising man
鋭敏で進取の気性に富んだ男
he had been taken on by a party of Englishmen
彼はイギリス人の一団に連れて行かれたのだ

they had come out to Ecuador to climb mountains
彼らは山に登るためにエクアドルにやって来ました
he replaced one of their guides who had fallen ill
彼は、病気になったガイドの一人と交代した
He had climbed many mountains of the world
彼は世界の多くの山に登ってきました
and then came the attempt at Mount Parascotopetl
そして、パラスコトペトル山での試みが始まりました
this was the Matterhorn of the Andes
これがアンデスのマッターホルンでした
here he was lost to the outer world
ここで彼は外の世界から消え去った
The story of that accident has been written a dozen times
あの事故の話は、何十回も書かれている
Pointer's narrative is the best account of events
ポインターの物語は、出来事の最良の説明です
He tells about the small group of mountaineers
彼は登山家の小さなグループについて語ります
he describes their difficult and almost vertical way up
彼は、その困難でほぼ垂直な道のりを描写しています
to the very foot of the last and greatest precipice
最後の、そして最大の断崖絶壁の麓まで
his account tells of how they built a night shelter
彼の話は、彼らが夜の避難所をどのように建てたかを語っています
amidst the snow upon a little shelf of rock
雪の中、小さな岩棚に
he tells the story with a touch of real dramatic power
彼は本当にドラマチックな力で物語を語っています
Nunez had gone from them in the night
ヌニェスは夜のうちに彼らから去った
They shouted, but there was no reply
彼らは叫んだが、返事はなかった

and for the rest of that night they slept no more
そして、その夜の残りは、もう眠れなかった
As the morning broke they saw the traces of his fall
夜が明けると、かれらは、イエスが倒れた痕跡を見た
It seems impossible he could have uttered a sound
彼が音を発することは不可能に思えます
He had slipped eastward
彼は東に滑り落ちたのだ
towards the unknown side of the mountain
山の知られざる側へ
far below he had struck a steep slope of snow
遥か下方では、雪の急斜面にぶつかった
and he must have tumbled all the way down it
そして、彼はその下まで転がり落ちたに違いありません
in the midst of a snow avalanche
雪崩の真っ只中
His track went straight to the edge of a frightful precipice
彼の足跡は恐ろしい崖っぷちにまっすぐ向かった
and beyond that everything was hidden
そして、その先はすべて隠されていました
Far below, and hazy with distance, they could see trees rising
遥か下方、遥か遠くに霞んで、木々が立ち上がっているのが見えた
out of a narrow, shut-in valley
狭い、閉じこもった谷から
the lost Country of the Blind
失われた盲人の国
But they did not know it was the Country of the Blind
しかし、彼らはそこが盲人の国だとは知りませんでした
they could not distinguish it from any other narrow valley
他の狭い谷と見分けがつかなかった

Unnerved by this disaster, they abandoned their attempt
この惨事に狼狽し、彼らはその試みを断念した
and Pointer was called away to the war
そしてポインターは戦争に召集されました
later he did make another attempt at the mountain
その後、彼は再び山に挑みました
To this day Parascotopetl lifts an unconquered crest
今日に至るまで、パラスコトペトルは征服されていない紋章を掲げています
and Pointer's shelter crumbles unvisited, amidst the snows
そしてポインターの避難所は、雪の中で、訪れることなく崩れ落ちます
And the man who fell survived...
そして、倒れた男は生き延びた...
At the end of the slope he fell a thousand feet
斜面の終わりに、彼は1000フィート落ちました
he came down in the midst of a cloud of snow
彼は雪雲の真っ只中に降りてきました
he landed on a snow-slope even steeper than the one above
彼は上の斜面よりもさらに急な雪の斜面に着地しました
Down this slope he was whirled
この坂道を下りて、彼は渦を巻いていた
the fall stunned him and he lost consciousness
落下して彼は気絶し、意識を失った
but not a bone in his body was broken
しかし、彼の体の骨は一本も折れていませんでした
finally, he fell down the gentler slopes
最後に、彼は緩やかな斜面を転げ落ちました
and at last he laid still
そしてとうとうじっと横たわった
he was buried amidst a softening heap of the white

snow
彼は柔らかな白い雪の山の中に埋葬された
the snow that had accompanied and saved him
彼を伴い、救った雪
He came to himself with a dim fancy that he was ill in bed
彼は、自分が病床に横たわっているのではないかというぼんやりとした空想を抱いていた
then he realized what had happened
その時、彼は何が起こったのかを悟った
with a mountaineer's intelligence he worked himself loose
登山家の知性で、彼は自分自身を解き放った
from the snow he saw the stars
雪の中から星が見えた
He rested flat upon his chest
彼は胸に伏せた
he wondered where he was
彼は自分がどこにいるのか不思議に思った
and he wondered what had happened to him
そして、自分に何が起こったのか不思議に思いました
He explored his limbs to check for damage
彼は自分の手足を探り、損傷がないか確認した
he discovered that several of his buttons were gone
彼は、いくつかのボタンがなくなっていることに気付きました
and his coat was turned over his head
そして、上着を頭からかぶせた
His knife had gone from his pocket
ポケットからナイフが抜け落ちていた
and his hat was lost too
帽子もなくしてしまいました
even though he had tied it under his chin
顎の下で縛っていたのに

He recalled that he had been looking for loose stones
彼は、ばらばらの石を探していたことを思い出しました
he wanted to raise his part of the shelter wall
彼はシェルターの壁の自分の部分を上げたかったのです
He realized he must have fallen
彼は自分が落ちたに違いないと悟った
and he looked up to see how far he had fallen
そして、どこまで落ちたか見上げた
the cliff was exaggerated by the ghastly light of the rising moon
崖は昇る月の恐ろしい光によって誇張されていた
the fall he had taken was tremendous
彼が受けた落下は凄まじいものだった
For a while he lay without moving
しばらくの間、彼は動かずに横たわっていた
he gazed blankly at the vast, pale cliff
彼はぼんやりと青白い崖を見つめていた
the mountain towered above him
頭上にそびえ立つ山
each moment it looked like it kept rising
一瞬一瞬、それは上昇し続けているように見えた
rising out of a subsiding tide of darkness
おさまりゆく闇の波から立ち上がる
Its phantasmal, mysterious beauty held him
その幻想的で神秘的な美しさが彼を捕らえました
and then he was seized with sobbing laughter
そして、すすり泣くような笑い声に襲われた
After a great interval of time he became more aware
かなりの時間が経った後、彼はより意識するようになった
he was laying near the lower edge of the snow
彼は雪の下端近くに横たわっていた
Below him the slope looked less steep
眼下には傾斜が緩やかに見えた

he saw the dark and broken appearance of rock-strewn turf
彼は岩が散らばった芝生の暗く壊れた外観を見た

He struggled to his feet, aching in every joint
彼はもがきながら立ち上がり、関節のあちこちが痛んだ

he got down painfully from the heaped loose snow
彼は積もった緩い雪から苦しそうに降りた

and he went downward until he was on the turf
そして、芝生の上に着くまで下って行きました

there he dropped beside a boulder
そこで彼は岩のそばに倒れました

he drank from the flask in his inner pocket
彼は内ポケットのフラスコから水を飲んだ

and he instantly fell asleep
そして、彼はすぐに眠りに落ちました

He was awakened by the singing of birds
彼は鳥のさえずりで目覚めました

they were in the trees far below
彼らは遥か下の木々の中にいた

He sat up and perceived he was on a little alp
彼は起き上がり、自分が少しアルプにいることに気づいた

at the foot of a vast precipice
広大な断崖絶壁のふもとに

a precipice that sloped only a little in the gully
峡谷で少しだけ傾斜した断崖絶壁

the path down which he and his snow had come
彼と彼の雪が下ってきた道

against him another wall of rock reared itself against the sky
彼の背後には、別の岩の壁が空に向かってそびえ立っていた

The gorge between these precipices ran east and west
この断崖絶壁の間の峡谷は東西に走っていました

and it was full of the morning sunlight
そして、朝の日差しがいっぱいでした

the sunlight lit the westward mass of fallen mountain
太陽の光がフォールンマウンテンの西向きの塊を照らした

he could see it closed the descending gorge
下降する峡谷を閉ざすのが見えた

Below there was a precipice equally steep
眼下には同じように急な断崖絶壁があった

behind the snow in the gully he found a sort of chimney-cleft
峡谷の雪の向こうに、煙突の裂け目のようなものを見つけた

it was dripping with snow-water
雪水が滴り落ちていた

a desperate man might be able to venture it
自暴自棄な男なら、思い切って挑戦できるかもしれない

He found it easier than it seemed
思ったより簡単だと感じた

and at last he came to another desolate alp
そしてとうとう、彼はまた荒涼としたアルプに来ました

there was a rock climb of no particular difficulty
特に難易度のないロッククライミングがありました

and he reached a steep slope of trees
そして、木々の急な斜面にたどり着きました

from here he was able to get his bearings
ここから、彼は自分の方向をつかむことができました

he turned his face up the gorge
彼は峡谷に顔を向けた

he saw it opened into green meadows
彼はそれが緑の牧草地に開かれているのを見た

there he saw quite distinctly the glimmer of some stone huts
そこには、石造りの小屋の明かりがはっきりと見えた

although the huts looked very strange
小屋はとても奇妙に見えましたが
even from a distance they didn't look like normal huts
遠くから見ても、普通の小屋には見えませんでした
At times his progress was like clambering along the face of a wall
時折、彼の歩みは壁をよじ登るようなものだった
and after a time the rising sun ceased to strike along the gorge
しばらくすると、朝日が峡谷に沿って沈むのをやめました
the voices of the singing birds died away
鳥のさえずりの声は消えた
and the air grew cold and dark
空気は冷たく暗くなった
But the distant valley with its houses got brighter
しかし、遠くの家々が立ち並ぶ谷間は明るくなってきた
He came to the edge of another cliff
彼は別の崖の端に来ました
he was an observant man
彼は観察力のある人でした
among the rocks he noted an unfamiliar fern
岩の間に見慣れないシダがいるのに気づいた
it seemed to clutch out of the crevices with intense green hands
それは強烈な緑色の手で隙間から掴み出しているようだった
He picked some of these new plants
彼はこれらの新しい植物のいくつかを選びました
and he gnawed their stalks
そして、その茎をかじった
they gave him strength and energy
彼らは彼に力とエネルギーを与えました
About midday he came out of the throat of the gorge

正午ごろ、彼は峡谷の喉から出てきた
and he came into the plain of the valley
そして、谷の平原に来られた
here he was in the sunlight again
ここで彼は再び太陽の光を浴びた
He was stiff and weary
彼はこわばり、疲れ果てていた
he sat down in the shadow of a rock
彼は岩の影に腰を下ろした
he filled up his flask with water from a spring
彼はフラスコに泉の水を入れた
and he drank the spring water
そして、その湧き水を飲んだ
he remained where he was for some time
彼はしばらくの間、その場にとどまった
before going to the houses he had decided to rest
家に行く前に、彼は休むことに決めました
They were very strange to his eyes
彼の目には、とても奇妙に映った
the more he looked around, the stranger the valley seemed
周りを見回せば見回すほど、谷は見知らぬものに見えた
The greater part of its surface was lush green meadow
その表面の大部分は青々とした緑の牧草地でした
it was starred with many beautiful flowers
たくさんの美しい花が咲いていました
extraordinary care had been taken for the irrigation
灌漑には細心の注意が払われていた
and there was evidence of systematic cropping
そして、体系的な作付けの証拠がありました
High up around the valley was a wall
渓谷の周囲には壁があった
there also appeared to be a circumferential water channel

また、円周方向に水路があるようにも見えました
the little trickles of water fed the meadow plants
小さな水滴が牧草地の植物に栄養を与えました
on the higher slopes above this were flocks of llamas
この上の高い斜面には、ラマの群れがいました
they cropped the scanty herbage
彼らは乏しい草を刈り取った
there were some shelters for the llamas
リャマのためのシェルターがいくつかありました
they had been built against the boundary wall
それらは境界の壁に対して建てられていた
The irrigation streams ran together into a main channel
灌漑用水路は一斉に主要水路に流れ込んでいた
these ran down the centre of the valley
これらは渓谷の中央を流れていた
and this was enclosed on either side by a wall chest high
そして、これは両側を胸の高さの壁で囲まれていました
This gave an urban quality to this secluded place
これにより、この人里離れた場所に都会的な品質が与えられました
a number of paths were paved with black and white stones
黒と白の石で舗装された道がいくつもありました
and the paths had a strange kerb at the side
そして、道の脇には奇妙な縁石がありました
this made it seem even more urban
これにより、さらに都会的に見えました
The houses of the central village were not randomly arranged
中央集落の家々は無造作に並べられていたわけではない
they stood in a continuous row
彼らは一列に並んで立っていた
and they were on both sides of the central street

そして、彼らは中央通りの両側にいました
here and there the odd walls were pierced by a door
あちこちに奇妙な壁に扉が突き刺さっていた
but there was not a single window to be seen
しかし、窓は一つも見えなかった
They were coloured with extraordinary irregularity
それらは異常な不規則性で着色されていました
they had been smeared with a sort of plaster
石膏のようなものが塗られていた
sometimes it was grey, sometimes drab
灰色で、くすんだ色でもあれば、くすんだ
sometimes it was slate-coloured
時にはスレート色だったりも
at other times it was dark brown
それ以外はこげ茶色でした
it was the wild plastering that first elicited the word blind
盲目という言葉を最初に引き起こしたのは、野生の漆喰でした
"whoever did this must have been as blind as a bat"
「誰がやったにせよ、コウモリのように盲目だったに違いない」
but also notable was their astonishing cleanness
しかし、その驚くべき清潔さも特筆すべき点でした
He descended down a steep place
急な坂道を下りた
and so he came to the wall
そして、彼は壁のところに来ました
this wall led the water around the valley
この壁は渓谷の周りの水を導いていました
and it ended near the bottom of the village
そして、それは村の底近くで終わりました
He could now see a number of men and women
彼は今や何人もの男女の姿を見ることができた

they were resting on piled heaps of grass
彼らは積み上げられた草の山の上で休んでいた
they seemed to be taking a siesta
彼らはシエスタをしているようでした
in the remoter part there were a number of children
辺鄙なところには、何人もの子供たちがいました
and then, nearer to him, there were three men
すると、その近くに、三人の男がいた
they were carrying pails along a little path
彼らは小さな小道に沿って桶を運んでいました
the paths ran from the wall towards the houses
道は壁から家に向かって走っていました
The men were clad in garments of llama cloth
男たちはラマの布の衣をまとっていた
and their boots and belts were of leather
彼らの長靴と帯は革でできていた
and they wore caps of cloth
彼らは布の帽子をかぶっていた
They followed one another in single file
それらは1つのファイルで互いにフォローしました
they yawned as they slowly walked
二人はあくびをしながらゆっくりと歩いていった
like men who have been up all night
徹夜した男たちのように
Their movement seemed prosperous and respectable
彼らの運動は繁栄し、立派に見えた
Nunez only hesitated for a moment
ヌニェスは一瞬だけ躊躇した
and then he came out from behind his rock
そして、彼は岩の後ろから出てきました
he gave vent to a mighty shout
彼は力強い叫び声をあげた
and his voice echoed round the valley
そして、その声は谷間に響き渡った

The three men stopped and moved their heads
三人の男は立ち止まり、頭を動かした
They seemed to be looking around
彼らは周りを見回しているようでした
They turned their faces this way and that way
彼らは顔をこっちに向け、こっちに向けました
and Nunez gesticulated wildly
とヌニェスは乱暴に身振り手振りをした
But they did not appear to see him
しかし、彼らは彼を見ていないようでした
despite all his waving and gestures
手を振ったり、身振り手振りをしたりしながらも
eventually they stood themselves towards the mountains
やがて二人は山の方へ立ち上がった
these were far away to the right
これらは右のはるか彼方にあった
and they shouted as if they were answering
と答えるかのように叫んだ
Nunez bawled again, and he gestured ineffectually
ヌニェスは再び吠え、彼は無意味なジェスチャーをした
"The fools must be blind," he said
「愚か者は盲目に違いない」と彼は言った
all the shouting and waving didn't help
叫んでも手を振っても役に立たなかった
so Nunez crossed the stream by a little bridge
そこでヌニェスは小さな橋で小川を渡った
he came through a gate in the wall
彼は壁の門をくぐって来た
and he approached them directly
そして、彼は直接彼らに近づきました
he was sure that they were blind
かれは、彼らが盲目であると確信していた
he was sure that this was the Country of the Blind

彼は、ここが盲人の国であると確信していました
the country of which the legends told
伝説が伝えた国
he had a sense of great adventure
彼は大いなる冒険心を持っていた
The three stood side by side
三人は並んで立っていた
but they did not look at him
しかし、彼らは彼を見なかった
however, their ears were directed towards him
しかし、彼らの耳は彼に向けられていました
they judged him by his unfamiliar steps
彼らは、その見慣れない足取りで彼を裁いた
They stood close together, like men a little afraid
二人は少し怯えた男のように寄り添って立っていた
and he could see their eyelids were closed and sunken
そして、彼らのまぶたが閉じられ、くぼんでいるのが見えた
as though the very balls beneath had shrunk away
まるで、その下のボールが縮んでしまったかのように
There was an expression near awe on their faces
彼らの顔には畏敬の念に近い表情が浮かんでいた
"A man," one said to the others
「男だ」と一人が言った
Nunez hardly recognized the Spanish
ヌニェスはスペイン人をほとんど認識していなかった
"A man it is. Or it a spirit"
「男だ。あるいは精霊か」
"he come down from the rocks"
「彼は岩から降りてくる」
Nunez advanced with the confident steps
ヌニェスは自信に満ちたステップで前進した
like a youth who enters upon life
人生に踏み込む若者のように

All the old stories of the lost valley
失われた谷のすべての古い物語
all the stories of the Country of the Blind
盲人の国のすべての物語
it all come back to his mind
歌詞の意味: すべては彼の心に戻ります。
and through his thoughts ran an old proverb
そして、彼の思考を通して古いことわざが走った
"In the Country of the Blind..."
「盲人の国では...」
"...the One-Eyed Man is King"
「...隻眼の男は王だ」
"In the Country of the Blind the One-Eyed Man is King"
「盲人の国では、隻眼の男が王様」
very civilly he gave them greeting
とても礼儀正しく挨拶をしました
He talked to them and used his eyes
彼は彼らに話しかけ、目を使いました
"Where does he come from, brother Pedro?" asked one
「ペドロ兄弟、彼はどこから来たのですか?」と一人が尋ねた
"from out of the rocks"
「岩の外から」
"I come from over the mountains," said Nunez
「私は山の向こうから来ました」とヌニェスは言った
"I'm from the country where where men can see"
「男が見える国から来た」
"I'm from a place near Bogota"
「ボゴタ近郊の出身です」
"there there are hundreds of thousands of people"
「そこには何十万人もの人々がいる」
"the city is so big it goes over the horizon"
「街は地平線の向こうまで広がっている」

"Sight?" muttered Pedro
「視力?」ペドロが呟いた
"He comes out of the rocks," said the second blind man
「あの人は岩から出てくるんだ」と二人目の盲人が言いました
The cloth of their coats was curiously fashioned
上着の布地は不思議な形をしていた
each patch was of a different sort of stitching
各パッチは異なる種類のステッチでした
They startled him by a simultaneous movement towards him
彼らは一斉に彼に向かって動いて彼を驚かせた
each of them had his hand outstretched
それぞれが手を伸ばしていた
He stepped back from the advance of these spread fingers
彼は広げた指の前進から一歩下がった
"Come hither," said the third blind man
「こっちへ来い」と三人目の盲人が言いました
and he followed Nunez' motion
そして彼はヌニェスの動きに従った
he quickly had hold of him
彼はすぐに彼を捕まえました
they held Nunez and felt him over
彼らはヌニェスを抱きかかえ、彼を抱きしめた
they said no word further until they were done
彼らは、それが終わるまで何も言わなかった
"Careful!" he exclaimed, with a finger in his eye
「気をつけろ!」彼は目に指を突っ込んで叫んだ
they had found a strange organ on him
彼らは彼に奇妙な器官を見つけたのです
"it has fluttering skin"
「肌がひらひらしている」
"it is very strange indeed"

「実に奇妙だ」
They went over it again
彼らは再びそれを調べた
"A strange creature, Correa," said the one called Pedro
「奇妙な生き物だ、コレア」ペドロと呼ばれた男が言った
"Feel the coarseness of his hair"
「彼の髪の毛のざらざら感を感じて」
"it's like a llama's hair"
「ラマの髪の毛みたいだね」
"Rough he is as the rocks that begot him," said Correa
「彼は彼を生んだ岩のようだ」とコレアは言った
and he investigated Nunez's unshaven chin
そしてヌニェスの髭を剃っていない顎を調べた
his hands were soft and slightly moist
彼の手は柔らかく、少し湿っていた
"Perhaps he will grow finer"
「もしかしたら、もっと元気になるかもしれない」
Nunez tried to free himself from their examination
ヌニェスは彼らの検査から自分を解放しようとした
but they had a firm grip on him
しかし、彼らは彼をしっかりと掴んでいた
"Careful," he said again "he speaks"
「気をつけろ」と彼は再び言った。
"we can be sure that he is a man"
「彼が男であることは確かだ」
"Ugh!" said Pedro, at the roughness of his coat
「うわぁ!」ペドロはコートのざらざらした様子に言った
"And you have come into the world?" asked Pedro
「それで、あなたはこの世に来たのですか?」とペドロは尋ねた
"I come from the world out there"
「私は外の世界から来ました」

"I come from over mountains and glaciers"
「山と氷河の向こうからやってきた」
"it is half-way to the sun"
「太陽まであと半分です」
"Out of the great, big world that goes down"
「消える大きな、大きな世界から」
"twelve days' journey to the sea"
「海への12日間の旅」
They scarcely seemed to heed him
かれらは、ほとんど彼の言葉に耳を傾けていないようだった
"Our fathers have told us of such things"
「私たちの先祖は、そのようなことを私たちに話しました」
"men may be made by the forces of Nature," said Correa
「人間は自然の力によって作られているのかもしれない」とコレアは言った
"Let us lead him to the elders," said Pedro
「長老たちのところに連れて行こう」とペドロは言った
"Shout first," said Correa
「まず叫べ」とコレアは言った
"the children might be afraid"
「子どもたちは怖いかもしれない」
"This is a marvellous occasion"
「これは素晴らしい機会です」
So they shouted to the others
それで、彼らは他の者たちに叫びました
Pedro took Nunez by the hand
ペドロはヌニェスの手を取った
and he lead him to the houses
そして、彼を家に連れて行きました
He drew his hand away
彼は手を引いた

"I can see," he said
「見える」と彼は言った
"to see?" said Correa
「見たい?」コレアは言った
"Yes, I can see with my eyes," said Nunez
「ええ、私の目で見ることができます」とヌニェスは言った
and he turned towards him
そして彼は彼の方を向いた
but he stumbled against Pedro's pail
しかし、彼はペドロのバケツにつまずいた
"His senses are still imperfect," said the third blind man
「彼の感覚はまだ不完全だ」と三人目の盲人が言った
"He stumbles, and talks unmeaning words"
「彼はつまずき、意味のない言葉を話す」
"Lead him by the hand"
「手を引いて」
"As you will" said Nunez
「お望みどおりに」とヌニェスは言った
and he was led along
そして、彼は導かれました
but he had to laugh at the situation
しかし、彼はその状況を笑うしかなかった
it seemed they knew nothing of sight
彼らは何も知らないようだった
"I will teach them soon enough," he thought to himself
「すぐに教えてやろう」と彼は心の中で思った
He heard people shouting
人々の叫び声が聞こえた
and he saw a number of figures gathering together
そして、何人もの人影が集まっているのが見えた
he saw them in the middle roadway of the village
彼は村の真ん中の車道で彼らを見た

all of it taxed his nerve and patience
そのすべてが彼の神経と忍耐に負担をかけました
there were more than he had anticipated
予想以上に多かった
this was the first encounter with the population
これが住民との最初の出会いでした
the people from the Country of the Blind
盲人の国の人々
The place seemed larger as he drew near to it
近づくにつれ、その場所は大きく見えた
and the smeared plasterings became even queerer
そして、汚れた漆喰はさらに奇妙になりました
a crowd of children and men and women came around him
子供や男女の群れが彼の周りにやって来ました
they all tried to hold on to him
彼らは皆、彼にしがみつこうとしました
they touched him with their soft and sensitive hands
彼らは柔らかく敏感な手で彼に触れました
not surprisingly, they smelled at him too
当然のことながら、彼らも彼の匂いを嗅いだ
and they listened at every word he spoke
そして、かれらは、イエスが話す一言一言に耳を傾けた
some of the women and girls had quite sweet faces
女性や少女の中には、とても甘い顔をしている人もいました
even though their eyes were shut and sunken
たとえ彼らの目が閉じられ、沈んでいたとしても
he thought this would make his stay more pleasant
そうすれば、滞在がもっと快適になると考えたのです
However, some of the maidens and children kept aloof
しかし、乙女や子供たちの中には、よそよそしい者もいました
they seemed to be afraid of him

彼らは彼を恐れているようでした
his voice seemed coarse and rude beside their softer notes
彼の声は、彼らの柔らかな音符の傍らで粗野で失礼に見えた
it is reasonable to say the crowd mobbed him
群衆が彼を暴徒化したと言うのは妥当です
but his three guides kept close to him
しかし、彼の3人のガイドは彼に近づいていました
they had taken some pride and ownership in him
彼らは彼にいくらかの誇りと所有権を持っていた
again and again they said, "A wild man out of the rocks"
彼らは何度も何度も「岩から出てきた野人」と言いました。
"Bogota," he said, "Over the mountain crests"
「ボゴタ」と彼は言った、「山の頂上を越えて」
"A wild man using wild words," said Pedro
「野蛮な言葉を使う野蛮な男だ」とペドロは言った
"Did you hear that, Bogota?"
「聞こえたか、ボゴタ?」
"His mind has hardly formed yet"
「彼の心はまだほとんど形成されていない」
"He has only the beginnings of speech"
「彼には言葉の始まりしかない」
A little boy nipped his hand
小さな男の子が彼の手を握った
"Bogota!" he said mockingly
「ボゴタ!」彼は嘲るように言った
"Aye! A city to your village"
「ああ!あなたの村に都市を」
"I come from the great world"
「私は大いなる世界からやってきた」
"the world where men have eyes and see"

「男が目と見る世界」
"His name's Bogota," they said
「彼の名前はボゴタです」と彼らは言った
"He stumbled," said Correa
「彼はつまずいた」とコレアは言った
"he stumbled twice as we came hither"
「ここに来るとき、彼は二度つまずいた」
"bring him in to the elders"
「彼を長老のところに連れて来なさい」
And they thrust him through a doorway
そして、彼らは彼を戸口から突き落とした
he found himself in a room as black as pitch
気がつくと、彼は真っ暗な部屋にいた
but slowly his eyes adjusted to the darkness
しかし、彼の目は徐々に暗闇に順応していった
at the far end a fire faintly glowed
その奥で、かすかに火が燃えていた
The crowd closed in behind him
群衆は彼の後ろに迫った
and they shut out any light that could have come from outside
そして、外から来る可能性のある光をシャットアウトします
before he could stop himself he had fallen
自分を止める間もなく、彼は倒れてしまった
he fell right into the lap of a seated man
彼は座っている男の膝の上に落ちた
and his arm struck the face of someone else
そして彼の腕が他の誰かの顔に当たった
he felt the soft impact of features
彼は機能の柔らかな影響を感じました
and he heard a cry of anger
そして、怒りの叫びを聞いた
for a moment he struggled against a number of hands

一瞬、彼は何人もの手と格闘した
all of them were clutching him
全員が彼を掴んでいた
but it was a one-sided fight
しかし、それは一方的な戦いでした
An inkling of the situation came to him
状況の予兆が彼に浮かんだ
and he decided to lay quiet
そして彼は静かに横たわることにした
"I fell down," he said
「私は倒れました」と彼は言った
"I couldn't see in this pitchy darkness"
「この真っ暗な闇の中では見えなかった」
There was a pause at what he had said
彼の言葉に一瞬の沈黙があった
he felt unseen persons trying to understand his words
目に見えない人が自分の言葉を理解しようとしているのを感じた
Then he heard the voice of Correa
その時、彼はコレアの声を聞いた
"He is but newly formed"
「彼は新しく形成されたに過ぎない」
"He stumbles as he walks"
「彼は歩きながらつまずく」
"and his speech mingles words that mean nothing"
「そして、彼の演説には、何の意味もない言葉が混ざっている」
Others also said things about him
他の人も彼について何かを言いました
they all confirmed they could not perfectly understand him
彼らは皆、イエスを完全に理解することはできないと認めた
"May I sit up?" he asked during a pause

「座ってもいいですか?」彼は間を置いて尋ねた
"I will not struggle against you again"
「もう二度とお前と戦わない」
the elders consulted, and let him rise
長老たちは相談し、彼を立ち上がらせた
The voice of an older man began to question him
年配の男の声が彼に問いかけ始めた
again, Nunez found himself trying to explain the world
ここでもまた、ヌニェスは世界を説明しようとしている自分に気づいた
the great world out of which he had fallen
彼が堕落した大いなる世界
he told them of the sky and mountains
彼は彼らに空と山のことを告げた
and he tried to convey other such marvels
そして、彼は他のそのような驚異を伝えようとしました
but the elders sat in darkness
しかし、長老たちは暗闇の中に座っていた
and they did not know of the Country of the Blind
彼らは盲人の国を知らなかった
if only he could show these elders
長老たちに見せてあげられればいいのに
but they believed and understood nothing
しかし、彼らは何も信じず、何も理解しませんでした
whatever he told them created confusion
彼が彼らに言ったことは何であれ、混乱を生んだ
it was all quite outside his expectations
それはすべて彼の予想をはるかに超えていました
They did not understand many of his words
かれらは、イエスの言葉の多くを理解していなかった
For generations these people had been blind
何世代にもわたって、これらの人々は盲目でした
and they had been cut off from all the seeing world

そして、彼らはすべての見る世界から切り離されていました
the names for all the things of sight had faded and changed
目に見えるものの名前は色あせて変わっていた
the story of the outer world had become a story
外界の話が物語になっていた
his world was just something people told their children
彼の世界は、人々が子供たちに話すものにすぎませんでした
and they had ceased to concern themselves with it
そして、かれらは、それについて気にするのをやめた
the only thing of interest was inside the rocky slopes
唯一興味を引いたのは、岩だらけの斜面の中でした
they lived only in their circling wall
彼らは周囲を囲む壁の中だけに住んでいた
Blind men of genius had arisen among them
彼らの中に天才的な盲人が現れた
they had questioned the old believes and traditions
彼らは古い信仰や伝統に疑問を抱いていた
and they had dismissed all these things as idle fancies
そして、かれらは、これらすべてのことを、くだらない空想として退けた
they replaced them with new and saner explanations
彼らはそれらを新しく、よりまともな説明に置き換えました
Much of their imagination had shrivelled with their eyes
彼らの想像力の多くは、彼らの目でしぼんでいた
their ears and finger-tips had gotten ever more sensitive
耳と指先がますます敏感になっていた
and with these they had made themselves new

imaginations
そして、これらによって、彼らは新しい想像力を創造したのである

Slowly Nunez realised the situation he was in
ヌニェスはゆっくりと、自分が置かれている状況に気づいた

he could not expect any reverence for his origin
かれは、自分の出自に対するいかなる畏敬の念も期待できなかった

his gifts were not as useful as he thought
彼の賜物は、彼が思っていたほど役に立つものではありませんでした

explaining sight was not going to be easy
視力の説明は容易ではなかった

his attempts had been quite incoherent
彼の試みは全く支離滅裂だった

he was deflated from his initial excitement
彼は最初の興奮からしぼんでいた

and he subsided into listening to their instruction
そして、かれは、彼らの指示に耳を傾けることに落ち着いた

the eldest of the blind men explained to him life
盲人の長男は彼に人生を説明しました

he explained to him philosophy and religion
彼は彼に哲学と宗教を説明しました

he described the origins of the world
彼は世界の起源を説明しました

(by this of course he meant the valley)
(もちろん、これは谷を意味していました)

first it had been an empty hollow in the rocks
最初は岩の空洞だった

first came inanimate things without the gift of touch
最初に現れたのは、触覚の賜物のない無生物でした

then came llamas and other creatures of little sense

その後、ラマや他の感覚の薄い生き物がやって来ました
when all had been put in place, men came
すべての準備が整うと、男たちがやって来た
and finally angels came to the world
そしてついに天使たちがこの世にやって来ました
one could hear the angels singing and making fluttering sounds
天使たちが歌い、羽ばたく音が聞こえる
but it was impossible to touch them
しかし、それらに触れることは不可能でした
this explanation first puzzled Nunez greatly
この説明は最初、ヌニェスを大いに困惑させた
but then he thought of the birds
しかし、その時、彼は鳥のことを思い浮かべた
He went on to tell Nunez how time had been divided
彼はヌニェスに、時間がどのように分割されたかを話した
there was the warm time and the cold time
暖かい時と寒い時がありました
of course these are the blind equivalents of day and night
もちろん、これらは昼と夜の盲目的な同等物です
he told how it was good to sleep in the warm
彼は暖かい中で眠るのがどんなに良かったかを話しました
he explained how it was better to work during the cold
寒い時期に作業した方が良いと説明してくれました
normally the whole town of the blind would now have been asleep
普通なら、盲人の町全体が眠りについたはずだ
but this special event kept them up
しかし、この特別なイベントが彼らを支え続けました
He said Nunez must have been specially created to learn

彼は、ヌニェスは学ぶために特別に作られたに違いないと言いました

and he was there to serve the wisdom they had acquired
そして、かれは、彼らが獲得した知恵に仕えるためにそこにいた

his mental incoherency was ignored, for the time being
彼の精神的な支離滅裂さは、当分の間無視された

and he was forgiven for his stumbling behaviour
そして、彼はつまずいた行動を赦されました

he was told to have courage in this world
彼はこの世で勇気を持てと言われました

and he was told to do his best to learn
そして、彼は学ぶために最善を尽くすように言われました

all the people in the doorway murmured encouragingly
戸口にいた人々は皆、励ましの言葉を呟いた

He said the night was far gone
彼は夜は遠い昔に過ぎ去ったと言った

(the blind call their day night)
(盲人は昼夜と呼ぶ)

so he encouraged everyone to go back to sleep
それで、彼はみんなに眠りに戻るように勧めました

He asked Nunez if he knew how to sleep
彼はヌニェスに、眠り方を知っているかと尋ねた

Nunez said he did know how to sleep
ヌニェスは、眠り方を知っていると言った

but that before sleep he wanted food
しかし、寝る前に食べ物が欲しかったのです

They brought him some of their food
彼らは彼に食べ物を持ってきました

llama's milk in a bowl and rough salted bread
ボウルに入ったラマのミルクと粗い塩漬けのパン

and they led him into a lonely place
そして、彼らは彼を寂しい場所に連れて行きました
so that he could eat out of their hearing
それは、彼が彼らの耳から食べられるようにするためです
afterwards he was allowed to slumber
その後、彼はまどろむことを許された
until the chill of the mountain evening roused them
山の夜の寒さが彼らを目覚めさせるまでは
and then they would begin their day again
そして、彼らは再び一日を始めるでしょう
But Nunez slumbered not at all
しかし、ヌニェスはまったくまどろんでいなかった
Instead, he sat up in the place where they had left him
その代わりに、彼は彼らが彼を置いていった場所に座りました
he rested his limbs, still sore from the fall
彼は手足を休めたが、まだ転倒の痛みが残っていた
and he turned everything over and over in his mind
そして、彼は心の中ですべてを何度も繰り返しました
the unanticipated circumstances of his arrival
彼の到着の予期せぬ状況
Every now and then he laughed
時折、彼は笑った
sometimes with amusement, and sometimes with indignation
時には面白がり、時には憤慨して
"Unformed mind!" he said, "Got no senses yet!"
「未熟な心!」と彼は言った、「まだ感覚がない!」
"little do they know what they're saying!"
「あいつらは何を言っているのか、ほとんどわかってないんだ!」
"they've been insulting their Heaven-sent King and master"

「彼らは天から遣わされた王と主人を侮辱している」
"I see I must bring them to reason"
「なるほど、私は彼らを理性に従わなければならない」
"Let me think about this..."
「ちょっと考えさせてください……」

He was still thinking when the sun set
太陽が沈んだとき、彼はまだ考えていた

Nunez had an eye for all beautiful things
ヌニェスはすべての美しいものを見抜く目を持っていた

he saw the glow upon the snow-fields and glaciers
彼は雪原と氷河の上の輝きを見た

on the mountains that rose about the valley on every side
四方を渓谷にそびえ立つ山々に

it was the most beautiful thing he had ever seen
それは彼が今まで見た中で最も美しいものだった

His eyes went over the inaccessible glory to the village
彼の目は、近づくことのできない村の栄光を見渡した

he looked over irrigated fields sinking into the twilight
彼は灌漑された田んぼが夕暮れに沈んでいくのを見渡した

suddenly a wave of emotion hit him
突然、感情の波が彼を襲った

he thanked God from the bottom of his heart
彼は心の底から神に感謝しました

"thank you for the power of sight you have given me"
「あなたが私に与えてくれた視力に感謝します」

He heard a voice calling to him
彼を呼ぶ声が聞こえた

it was coming from the village
それは村から来ていた

"ahoi-hoi, Bogota! Come hither!"
「アホイホイ、ボゴタ!こっちに来い!」

At that he stood up, smiling
その時、彼は微笑みながら立ち上がった
He would show these people once and for all!
彼はこれらの人々をきっぱりと見せます!
"they will learn what sight can do for a man!"
「彼らは、視覚が人間に何ができるかを学ぶでしょう!」
"I shall make them seek me"
「わたしは彼らにわたしを捜し求めさせる」
"but they shall not be able to find me"
「しかし、彼らはわたしを見つけることができないであろう」
"You move not, Bogota," said the voice
「動くな、ボゴタ」と声がした
at this he laughed, without making a noise
これを見て、彼は音を立てずに笑った
he made two stealthy steps from the path
彼は小道からこっそりと二歩進んだ
"Trample not on the grass, Bogota"
「草を踏みにじるな、ボゴタ」
"wondering off the path is not allowed"
「道を外れることは許されない」
Nunez had scarcely heard the sound he made himself
ヌニェスは、自分が発した音をほとんど聞いていなかった
He stopped where he was, amazed
彼は驚いてその場で立ち止まりました
the owner of the voice came running up the path
声の主が小道を駆け上がってきた
and he stepped back into the pathway
そして彼は小道に足を踏み入れた
"Here I am," he said
「ここにいるよ」と彼は言った
the blind man was not impressed with Nunez's antics

盲目の男はヌニェスのふざけた態度に感銘を受けなかった

"Why did you not come when I called you?"
「私が呼んだのに、どうして来なかったの?」

"Must you be led like a child?"
「子供みたいに導かれなきゃいけないの?」

"Cannot you hear the path as you walk?"
「歩いていると道の音が聞こえませんか?」

Nunez laughed at the ridiculous questions
ヌニェスは馬鹿げた質問に笑った

"I can see it," he said
「私には見える」と彼は言った

the blind man paused for a moment
盲目の男は一瞬立ち止まった

"There is no such word as see"
「見るような言葉はない」

"Cease this folly and follow the sound of my feet"
「この愚行をやめて、私の足音に従ってください」

Nunez followed the blind man, a little annoyed
ヌニェスは少し苛立って盲目の男の後を追った

"My time will come," he said to himself
「私の時が来る」と彼は自分に言い聞かせた

"You'll learn," the blind man answered
「お前は学ぶだろう」と盲目の男は答えた

"There is much to learn in the world"
「世界には学ぶべきことがたくさんある」

"Has no one told you?" asked Nunez
「誰も教えてくれなかったのか?」ヌニェスが尋ねた

"In the Country of the Blind the One-Eyed Man is King"
「盲人の国では、隻眼の男が王様」

"What is blind?" asked the blind man, over his shoulder
「盲目って何だ?」と盲目の男は肩越しに尋ねた

by now four days had passed
この時までに4日が経過していた
even on the fifth day nothing had changed
5日目になっても何も変わっていなかった
the King of the Blind was still incognito
盲人の王はまだお忍びでした
he was still a clumsy and useless stranger among his subjects
彼はまだ不器用で役に立たない見知らぬ人でした
he found it all much more difficult than he thought
彼は、自分が思っていたよりもずっと難しいことに気づきました
how could he proclaim himself king to these blind people??
どうして彼はこの盲人に自分を王と宣言することができようか。
he was left to meditated his coup d'etat
彼はクーデターを瞑想するしかなかった
in the meantime he did what he was told
その間、彼は言われたとおりにしました
he learnt the manners and customs of the Country of the Blind
彼は盲人の国の風俗や習慣を学びました
working at night he found particularly irksome
夜の作業は特に不愉快だった
this was going to be the first thing he changed
これが彼が最初に変えたことになる
They led a simple and laborious life
彼らは質素で骨の折れる生活を送っていました
but they had all the elements of virtue and happiness
しかし、彼らは美徳と幸福のすべての要素を持っていました
They toiled, but not oppressively
かれらは、労苦しはしたが、抑圧的ではなかった

they had food and clothing sufficient for their needs
彼らは自分たちの必要を満たすのに十分な食料と衣服を持っていました
they had days and seasons of rest
彼らには休息の日と季節があった
they enjoyed music and singing
彼らは音楽と歌を楽しんだ
there was love among them
彼らの間には愛があった
and there were little children
そして、小さな子供たちがいました
It was marvellous to see their confidence and precision
彼らの自信と正確さを見るのは素晴らしいことでした
they went about their ordered world efficiently
彼らは秩序ある世界を効率的に動き回った
Everything had been made to fit their needs
すべてが彼らのニーズに合うように作られていました
each paths had a constant angle to the other
各パスは、他のパスに対して一定の角度を持っていました
each kerb was distinguished by a special notch
各縁石は特別な切り欠きによって区別されました
all obstacles and irregularities had been cleared away
すべての障害と不規則性が取り除かれました
all their methods arose naturally from their special needs
彼らの方法はすべて、彼らの特別なニーズから自然に生まれました
and their procedures made sense to their abilities
そして、彼らの手順は彼らの能力に意味がありました
their senses had become marvellously acute
彼らの感覚は驚くほど鋭くなっていた
they could hear and judge the slightest gesture
彼らはわずかな仕草を聞いて判断することができました

even if the man was a dozen paces away
たとえその男が十数歩離れていたとしても
they could hear the very beating of his heart
心臓の鼓動が聞こえる
Intonation and touch had long replaced expression and gesture
イントネーションとタッチは、長い間、表情とジェスチャーに取って代わっていました
they were handy with the hoe and spade
彼らは鍬と鋤で便利でした
and they moved as free and confident as any gardener
そして、彼らは庭師のように自由で自信を持って動きました
Their sense of smell was extraordinarily fine
彼らの嗅覚は並外れて優れていた
they could distinguish individual differences as quickly as a dog can
犬と同じくらい早く個体差を見分けることができました
and they went about the tending of llamas with ease and confidence
そして、彼らは、楽々と自信を持ってラマの世話をしました
a day came Nunez sought to assert himself
ある日、ヌニェスは自己主張をしようとした
but he quickly realized his underestimation
しかし、彼はすぐに自分の過小評価に気づきました
and he learned how confident their movements could be
そして、彼らの動きがいかに自信に満ちているかを学びました
he rebelled only after he had tried persuasion
かれは、説得を試みた後にのみ反抗した
on several occasions he had tried to tell them of sight
かれは、何度か彼らに光景を伝えようとした

"Look you here, you people," he said
「ほら、お前ら」と彼は言った

"There are things you people do not understand in me"
「お前らには俺には理解できないことがある」

Once or twice one or two of them listened to him
一度か二度、一人か二人が彼の話を聞いた

they sat with their faces downcast
彼らは顔を伏せて座っていた

their ears were turned intelligently towards him
彼らの耳は知的に彼に向けられた

and he did his best to tell them what it was to see
そして、彼は彼らにそれが何であるかを伝えるために最善を尽くしました

Among his hearers was a girl
彼の聴衆の中に一人の少女がいた

her eyelids were less red and sunken
瞼の赤みは減り、窪んでいた

one could almost imagine she was hiding eyes
彼女が目を隠しているのが想像できるほどです

he especially hoped to persuade her
彼は特に彼女を説得することを望んでいた

He spoke of the beauties of sight
彼は視覚の美しさについて話しました

he spoke of watching the mountains
彼は山を眺めていたと話した

he told them of the sky and the sunrise
彼は彼らに空と日の出を告げた

and they heard him with amused incredulity
そして、かれらは、面白がって信じられない思いでイエスを聞いた

but that eventually became condemnatory
しかし、それはやがて非難されるようになった

They told him there were no mountains at all
山は全くないと言われた

they told him only the llamas go to the rocks
彼らは彼に、岩に行くのはラマだけだと言いました
they graze their grass there at the edge
彼らは端で草を食んでいます
and that is the end of the world
そして、それは世界の終わりです
from there the roof rises over the universe
そこから、宇宙の上に屋根がそびえ立つ
only the dew and the avalanches fell from there
露と雪崩だけがそこから落ちてきた
he maintained stoutly the world had neither end nor roof
彼は、世界には終わりも屋根もないと頑なに主張した
everything they thought about the world was wrong, he told them
彼らが世界について考えることはすべて間違っている、と彼は彼らに言いました
but they said his thoughts were wicked
しかし、彼らは彼の考えは邪悪だと言いました
his descriptions of sky and clouds and stars were hideous to them
空や雲や星についての彼の描写は、彼らにとって恐ろしいものでした
a terrible blankness in the place of the smooth roof of the world
世界の滑らかな屋根の代わりに恐ろしい空白
it was an article of faith with them
それは彼らにとって信仰箇条であった
they believed the cavern roof was exquisitely smooth to the touch
彼らは、洞窟の屋根が絶妙に滑らかな手触りであると信じていました
he saw that in some manner he shocked them
彼は、何らかの方法で彼らに衝撃を与えたのを見ました

and he gave up that aspect of the matter altogether
そして、彼はその問題の側面を完全にあきらめました
instead, he tried to show them the practical value of sight
その代わりに、彼は彼らに視覚の実際的な価値を示そうとしました
One morning he saw Pedro on path Seventeen
ある朝、彼はペドロが17番道にいるのを見た
he was coming towards the central houses
彼は中央の家々に向かって来ていた
but he was still too far away for hearing or scent
しかし、彼はまだ遠くすぎて、耳も匂いもつかなかった
"In a little while," he prophesied, "Pedro will be here"
「しばらくすれば、ペドロはここに来るだろう」と彼は予言した
An old man remarked that Pedro had no business on path Seventeen
老人は、ペドロは17番道に用事がないと言った
and then, as if in confirmation, Pedro changed paths
そして、確認するかのように、ペドロは道を変えた
with nimble paces he went towards the outer wall
軽快な足取りで、彼は外壁へと向かった
They mocked Nunez when Pedro did not arrive
彼らはペドロが到着しなかったとき、ヌニェスを嘲笑した
he tried to clear his character by asking Pedro
彼はペドロに尋ねることによって彼の性格をクリアしようとしました
but Pedro denied the allegations
しかし、ペドロは疑惑を否定した
and afterwards he was hostile to him
その後、彼は彼に敵対的になった
Then he convinced them to let him go
そして、彼を手放すように彼らを説得しました

"let me go up the sloping meadows to the wall"
「坂道の草原を壁まで登らせてください」
"let me take with me one willing individual"
「一人の意欲的な個人を連れて行かせてください」
"I will describe all that is happening among the houses"
「家々の間で起きていることをすべて話します」
He noted certain goings and comings
彼は、ある種の出入りに気づいた
but these things were not important to these people
しかし、これらのことはこれらの人々にとって重要ではありませんでした
they cared for what happened inside the windowless houses
彼らは窓のない家の中で何が起こったのかを気にかけました
of those things he could neither see, nor tell
彼は見ることも、語ることもできなかったものについて、
his attempt had failed again
彼の試みは再び失敗した
they could not repress their ridicule
かれらは、嘲笑を抑えることができなかった
and finally Nunez resorted to force
そしてついにヌニェスは武力に訴えた
He thought of seizing a spade
彼はスペードをつかむことを考えた
he could smite one or two of them to earth
そのうちの1つか2つを地上に叩きつけることができる
in fair combat he could show the advantage of eyes
正々堂々とした戦闘では、彼は目の優位性を示すことができた
He went so far with that resolution as to seize his spade

彼はその決意を固め、鋤を握りしめた
but then he discovered a new thing about himself
しかし、その後、彼は自分自身について新しいことを発見しました
it was impossible for him to hit a blind man in cold blood
盲目の男を冷血に殴ることは不可能だった
holding the spade, he hesitated for a moment
スペードを握りしめながら、彼は一瞬躊躇した
all of them had become aware that he had snatched up the spade
彼らは皆、彼がスペードをひったくったことに気づいていました
They stood alert, with their heads on one side
彼らは警戒を怠らず、頭を片側に向けて立っていた
they cautiously bent their ears towards him
彼らは用心深く彼に耳を傾けた
and they waited for what he would do next
そして、かれらは、イエスが次に何をするかを待っていた
"Put that spade down," said one
「その鋤を置け」と一人が言った
and he felt a sort of helpless horror
そして、彼は一種のどうしようもない恐怖を感じた
he could not come to their obedience
かれは、彼らの従順に来ることができなかった
he thrust one backwards against a house wall
彼は一人を家の壁に後ろ向きに押し付けた
and he fled past him, and out of the village
そして、イエスのそばを通り過ぎて、村を出ました
he went over one of their meadows
かれは彼らの牧草地の1つを越えた
but of course he trampled grass behind him
しかし、もちろん彼は彼の後ろの草を踏みつけました

he sat down by the side of one of their ways
彼は彼らの道の脇に腰を下ろした
he felt something of the buoyancy in him
彼は自分の中に浮力のようなものを感じた
all men feel it in the beginning of a fight
すべての男性は、戦いの初めにそれを感じます
but he felt more perplexity than anything
しかし、彼は何よりも当惑を感じた
he began to realise something else about himself
彼は自分自身について何か別のことに気づき始めました
you cannot fight happily with creatures of a different mental basis
精神基盤の異なる生き物と楽しく戦うことはできません
Far away he saw a number of men carrying spades and sticks
遠くに、鋤と棒を持った男たちが何人もいるのが見えた
they were coming out of the streets and houses
彼らは通りや家々から出てきていた
together they made a line across the paths
二人は一緒に道を横切る線を作った
and they line was coming towards him
そして、彼らは彼の方へ向かってきていた
They advanced slowly, speaking frequently to one another
二人はゆっくりと進み、頻繁に話しかけた
again and again they stopped and sniff the air
何度も何度も立ち止まり、空気の匂いを嗅いだ
The first time they did this Nunez laughed
初めてこれをやったとき、ヌニェスは笑った
But afterwards he did not laugh
しかし、その後、彼は笑わなかった
One found his trail in the meadow grass
一人は草原の草むらに自分の足跡を見つけた
he came stooping and feeling his way along it

彼は身をかがめて、それに沿って自分の道を感じながらやって来ました

For five minutes he watched the slow extension of the line
5分間、彼は列がゆっくりと伸びていくのを見つめていた

his vague disposition to do something forthwith became frantic
すぐに何かをしたいという彼の漠然とした気質は、必死になった

He stood up and paced towards the wall
彼は立ち上がり、壁に向かって歩いた

he turned, and went back a little way
彼は踵を返し、少し戻って行った

they all stood in a crescent, still and listening
彼らは皆、三日月形に立って、じっと耳を傾けていた

He also stood still, gripping his spade
彼もまた立ち止まり、鋤を握りしめていた

Should he attack them?
彼は彼らを攻撃すべきですか?

The pulse in his ears ran into a rhythm:
耳の鼓動がリズムを刻んだ。

"In the Country of the Blind the One-Eyed Man is King"
「盲人の国では、隻眼の男が王様」

"In the Country of the Blind the One-Eyed Man is King"
「盲人の国では、隻眼の男が王様」

"In the Country of the Blind the One-Eyed Man is King"
「盲人の国では、隻眼の男が王様」

He looked back at the high and unclimbable wall
彼は高くて登れない壁を振り返った

and he looked at the approaching line of seekers

そして彼は近づいてくる求道者の列を見た
others were now coming out of the street of houses too
他の者達も今や家々の通りから出てきていた
"Bogota!" called one, "Where are you?"
「ボゴタ!」と一人が叫んだ、「どこにいるんだ?」
He gripped his spade even tighter
彼は鋤をさらに強く握りしめた
and he went down the meadow towards the place of habitations
そして、草原を下って住まいの所に向かった
where he moved they converged upon him
彼が動いたところに、彼らは彼に集まった
"I'll hit them if they touch me," he swore
「触られたら殴る」と彼は誓った
"by Heaven, I will. I'll hit them"
「天にかけて、わたしはそうします。殴ってやる」
He called aloud, "Look here you people"
彼は大声で「ここを見ろ、お前たち」と呼びかけた。
"I'm going to do what I like in this valley!"
「この谷で好きなことをやる!」
"Do you hear? I'm going to do what I like"
「聞こえますか?好きなことをやる」
"and I will go where I like"
「好きなところへ行きます」
They were moving in upon him quickly
奴らは素早く彼に近づいてきた
they were groping at everything, yet moving rapidly
彼らはあらゆるものを手探りで探していたが、それでも素早く動いていた
It was like playing blind man's bluff
それは盲目の男のブラフを演じるようなものでした
but everyone was blindfolded except one
しかし、一人を除いて全員が目隠しをされていました
"Get hold of him!" cried one

「あいつを捕まえろ!」と一人が叫んだ
He realized a group of men had surrounded him
彼は男たちの集団が自分を取り囲んでいることに気づいた

suddenly he felt he must be active and resolute
突然、彼は自分が積極的で毅然としていなければならないと感じました

"You people don't understand," he cried
「お前らには理解できない」と彼は叫んだ

his voice was meant to be great and resolute
彼の声は偉大で毅然としたものでした

but his voice broke and carried no power
しかし、その声は途切れ、何の力も持たなかった

"You are all blind and I can see"
「あなたはみんな盲目で、私には見える」

"Leave me alone!" he tried to command
「放っておけ!」彼は命じようとした

"Bogota! Put down that spade and come off the grass!"
「ボゴタ!その鋤を置いて、草から降りなさい!」

the order was grotesque in its familiarity
その教団は、その親しみやすさにおいてグロテスクだった

and it produced a gust of anger in him
そして、それは彼の中に怒りの突風を生み出しました

"I'll hurt you," he said, sobbing with emotion
「お前を傷つけてやる」と彼は言い、感情にすすり泣いた

"By Heaven, I'll hurt you! Leave me alone!"
「天にかけて、お前を傷つけてやる!ほっといてくれ!」

He began to run without knowing where to run
どこを走ればいいのかわからず走り出した

He ran away from the nearest blind man
彼は一番近くにいた盲人から逃げました

because it was a horror to hit him

彼を殴るのが恐ろしかったからです
He made a dash to escape from their closing ranks
彼は彼らの接近戦から逃れるためにダッシュした
in one place the gap was a little wider
ある場所では、ギャップが少し広がっていました
the men on the sides quickly perceived what was happening
両脇の男たちはすぐに何が起こっているのかを察知した
they quickly rushed in to close the gap
彼らはすぐにギャップを埋めるために駆けつけました
He sprang forward, and saw he would be caught
彼は前に跳び、捕まるのを悟った
and whoosh! the spade had struck
そしておっと!スペードが打たれたのだ
He felt the soft thud of hand and arm
彼は手と腕の柔らかな音を感じた
and the man was down with a yell of pain
男は苦痛の叫び声を上げて倒れた
and he was through the gap
そして、彼はそのギャップを通り抜けた
he was close to the street of houses again
彼は再び家々の通りに近づいた
the blind men were whirling their spades and stakes
盲目の男たちは鋤と杭を振り回していた
and they were running with a new swiftness
そして、彼らは新しい速さで走っていた
He heard steps behind him just in time
背後で足音が聞こえたのは、ちょうどその時だった
a tall man was rushing towards him
背の高い男が彼に向かって突進してきた
he was swiping his spade at the sound of him
彼はその音にスペードを振り回していた
Nunez lost his nerve this time
ヌニェスはこの時、神経を失った

he could not hit another blind man
彼は他の盲人を殴ることができなかった
he hurled his spade next to his antagonist
彼はスペードを敵の隣に投げつけた
the tall man whirled about from where he heard the noise
長身の男は、物音が聞こえた方からくるりと回った
and Nunez fled, yelling as he dodged another
ヌニェスは叫びながら逃げ出し、もう一人をかわした
He was panic-stricken by this point
この時点で彼はパニックに陥っていた
almost blindly, he ran furiously to and fro
ほとんど盲目的に、彼は猛烈にあちこち走った
he dodged when there was no need to dodge
かわす必要のないのにかわした
in his anxiety he tried to see every side of him at once
不安の中で、彼は自分のあらゆる側面を一度に見ようとしました
for a moment he had fallen down
一瞬、彼は倒れた
of course the followers heard his fall
勿論、信者達は彼の堕落を聞いた
he caught a glimpse of something in the circumferential wall
彼は周囲の壁に何かを垣間見た
a little gap between the wall
壁と壁の間のちょっとした隙間
he set off in a wild rush for it
彼はそれを求めて猛烈な勢いで出発した
he had stumbled across the bridge
彼は橋をよろめきながら渡ったのだ
and he clambered a little along the rocks
そして、岩に沿って少しよじ登りました
a surprised young llama went leaping out of sight

驚いた若いラマが飛び跳ねて見えなくなった
and then he lay down, sobbing for breath
そして横になり、息を切らしてすすり泣いた
And so his coup d'etat came to an end
こうして彼のクーデターは終結した
He stayed outside the wall of the valley of the blind
彼は盲人の谷の壁の外にとどまった
for two nights and days he was without food or shelter
二日二晩、彼は食べ物も住む場所もなかった
and he meditated upon the unexpected
そして、思いがけない出来事について瞑想した
During these meditations he repeated his motto frequently
これらの瞑想の間、彼は頻繁に彼のモットーを繰り返しました
"In the Country of the Blind the One-Eyed Man is King"
「盲人の国では、隻眼の男が王様」
He thought chiefly of ways of conquering these people
かれは、主にこれらの人々を征服する方法を考えた
and it grew clear that no practicable way was possible
そして、実行可能な方法がないことが明らかになりました
He had brought no weapons with him
彼は武器を持っていなかった
and now it would be hard to get any
そして今、それを手に入れるのは難しいでしょう
his civilized manner had not left him
彼の文明的な態度は彼から離れていなかった
there was no way he could assassinate a blind man
盲目の男を暗殺できるはずがない
Of course, if he did that, he could dictate the terms
もちろん、そうすれば、彼は条件を指示することができます

he could threaten them with further assassinations
彼はさらなる暗殺で彼らを脅すことができる
But, sooner or later he must sleep!
しかし、遅かれ早かれ彼は眠らなければなりません！
He tried to find food among the pine trees
彼は松の木の間で食べ物を見つけようとしました
at night the frost fell over the valley
夜になると、霜が谷に降りました
to be comfortable he slept under pine boughs
快適に過ごすために、彼は松の枝の下で眠りました
he thought about catching a llama, if he could
できることならラマを捕まえようと考えた
perhaps he could hammer it with a stone
もしかしたら、石で叩くことができるかもしれない
and then he could eat some of it
そして、彼はそれを少し食べることができました
But the llamas had doubt of him
しかし、ラマたちは彼を疑っていました
they regarded him with distrustful brown eyes
彼らは不信の茶色の目で彼を見た
and they spat at him when he came near
そして、イエスが近づくと、彼らはイエスに唾を吐きかけた
Fear came on him the second day
2日目に恐怖が襲ってきた
he was taken by fits of shivering
彼は震えの発作に襲われた
Finally he crawled back down the wall
とうとう彼は壁を這い下りた
and he went back into the Country of the Blind
そして、盲人の国に帰って行った
he shouted until two blind men came out to the gate
二人の盲人が門に出てくるまで、彼は叫びました
and he talked to him, negotiating his terms

そして、彼は彼に話しかけ、条件を交渉した
"I had gone mad," he said
「気が狂いそうだった」と彼は言った
"But I was only newly made"
「でも、私は新しくできただけなのに」
They said that was better
彼らはその方が良いと言いました
He told them he was wiser now
彼は彼らに、今はもっと賢くなったと言いました
and he repented of all he had done
そして、彼は自分のしたことをすべて悔い改めた
Then he wept without reserve
それから彼は惜しみなく泣きました
because he was very weak and ill now
なぜなら、彼は今、とても弱っていて、病気だったからです
they took that as a favourable sign
彼らはそれを好意的な兆候として受け止めました
They asked him if he still thought he could see
彼らは彼に、まだ見えると思うかと尋ねた
"No," he said, "That was folly"
「いや、あれは愚かだった」と彼は言った
"The word means nothing, less than nothing!"
「この言葉は、何の意味も持たない、無以下だ!」
They asked him what was overhead
彼らは彼に頭上に何があるのか尋ねました
"About ten times ten the height of a man"
「男の身長の10倍くらい」
"there is a roof above the world of rock"
「岩の世界の上に屋根がある」
"it is very, very smooth"
「とても、とてもスムーズです」
"So smooth, so beautifully smooth"
「とても滑らかで、とても美しく滑らかです」

He burst again into hysterical tears
彼は再びヒステリックに涙を流した
"Before you ask me any more, give me some food"
「これ以上聞かないうちに、食べ物をくれ」
"or else I shall die!"
「さもないと死んでしまう!」
He expected dire punishments
彼は悲惨な罰を期待していた
but these blind people were capable of toleration
しかし、これらの盲人は寛容でした
his rebellion was just more proof of his idiocy
彼の反逆は、彼の愚かさのさらなる証拠に過ぎなかった
they hardly needed more evidence for his inferiority
かれらは、イエスの劣等性について、これ以上の証拠をほとんど必要としなかった
as a punishment he was whipped some
罰として、彼は鞭で打たれました
and they appointed him to do the heaviest work
そして、彼らは彼を最も重い仕事に任命した
Nunez could see no other way of surviving
ヌニェスは他に生き延びる方法を見出せなかった
so he submissively did what he was told
それで、彼は言われたことを従順に実行しました
he was ill for some days
彼は数日間病気だった
and they nursed him kindly
そして、彼らは彼を親切に看病しました
that refined his submission
それは彼の提出物を洗練させました
but they insisted on him lying in the dark
しかし、彼らは彼が暗闇に横たわっていると主張しました
that was a great misery to him
それは彼にとって大きな悲惨さでした

blind philosophers came and talked to him
盲目の哲学者たちがやってきて、彼に話しかけた
they spoke of the wicked levity of his mind
かれらは、イエスの心の邪悪な軽薄さについて語った
and they retold the story of creation
そして、彼らは創造の物語を語り直した
they explained further how the world was structured
彼らはさらに、世界がどのように構成されているかを説明しました
and soon Nunez had doubts about what he thought he knew
そしてすぐにヌニェスは、自分が知っていると思っていることに疑問を抱くようになった
perhaps he really was the victim of hallucination
もしかしたら、本当に幻覚の犠牲者だったのかもしれない
and so Nunez became a citizen of the Country of the Blind
こうしてヌニェスは盲人の国の市民となった
and these people ceased to be a generalised people
そして、これらの人々は、一般化された民族であることをやめた
they became individualities to him
それらは彼にとって個性となった
and they grew familiar to him
そして、彼らは彼に親しみを抱くようになりました
the world beyond the mountains slowly faded
山の向こうの世界がゆっくりと消えていく
more and more it became remote and unreal
どんどん遠くて非現実的になっていきました
There was Yacob, his master
そこには師匠のヤコブがいた
he was a kindly man when not annoyed
彼は、イライラしていないときは親切な人でした

there was Pedro, Yacob's nephew
ヤコブの甥であるペドロがいました
and there was Medina-sarote
そしてメディナ・サローテがあった
she was the youngest daughter of Yacob
彼女はヤコブの末娘でした
she was little esteemed in the world of the blind
彼女は盲人の世界ではほとんど尊敬されていなかった
because she had a clear-cut face
顔がはっきりしていたから
and she lacked any satisfying glossy smoothness
そして、満足のいく艶やかな滑らかさを欠いていた
these are the blind man's ideal of feminine beauty
これらは、盲人の理想とする女性的な美しさです
but Nunez thought her beautiful at first sight
しかし、ヌニェスは一目見て彼女を美しいと思った
and now she was the most beautiful thing in all the world
そして今、彼女はこの世で最も美しいものだった
her features were not common in the valley
彼女の特徴は渓谷では一般的ではなかった
her closed eyelids were not sunken and red
閉じた瞼は窪んではおらず、赤くもなかった
but they lay as though they might open again at any moment
しかし、それらは今にも開き直りそうな勢いで横たわっていた
she had long eyelashes, which were considered a grave disfigurement
睫毛が長く、重篤な醜態とされた
and her voice was weak compared to the others
そして、彼女の声は他の人に比べて弱かった
so it did not satisfy the acute hearing of the young men
そのため、若い男性の鋭い聴覚を満足させませんでした

And so she had no lover
だから、彼女には恋人がいなかった
Nunez thought a lot about Medina-sarote
ヌニェスはメディナ・サローテについて多くのことを考えた
he thought perhaps he could win her
彼は彼女を勝ち取ることができるかもしれないと思った
and then he would be resigned to live in the valley
そして、彼は谷に住むことを諦めるでしょう
he could be happy for the rest of his days
彼は残りの日々を幸せに過ごすことができる
he watched her whenever he could
彼はできる限り彼女を見守った
and he found opportunities of doing her little services
そして、彼は彼女のささやかな奉仕をする機会を見つけました
he also found that she observed him
彼はまた、彼女が彼を観察していることに気づきました
Once at a rest-day gathering he noticed it
ある休息日の集まりで、彼はそれに気づいた
they sat side by side in the dim starlight
二人は薄暗い星明かりの中で並んで座っていた
the music was sweet and his hand came upon hers
音楽は甘美で、彼の手が彼女の上に来た
and he dared to clasp her hand
そして、彼は思い切って彼女の手を握りしめた
Then, very tenderly, she returned his pressure
そして、とても優しく、彼の圧力を返しました
And one day they were at their meal in the darkness
そしてある日、二人は暗闇の中で食事をしていました
he felt her hand very softly seeking him
彼は彼女の手がとても優しく彼を求めているのを感じた
as it chanced, the fire leapt just at that moment
偶然にも、その瞬間に火が飛び跳ねた

and he saw the tenderness in her
そして、彼は彼女の優しさを見た
He sought to speak to her
彼は彼女に話しかけようとした
He went to her one day when she was sitting
ある日、彼女が座っているとき、彼は彼女のところに行きました
she was in the summer moonlight, weaving
彼女は夏の月明かりの中で、機織りをしていた
The light made her a thing of silver and mystery
その光は彼女を銀と神秘のものにした
He sat down at her feet
彼は彼女の足元に腰を下ろした
and he told her he loved her
そして、彼は彼女を愛していると言いました
and he told her how beautiful she seemed to him
そして、彼女がどんなに美しく見えるかを彼女に話しました
He had a lover's voice
彼には恋人の声が聞こえた
he spoke with a tender reverence that came near to awe
彼は畏敬の念に近い優しい畏敬の念を込めて話した
she had never before been touched by adoration
彼女はそれまで一度も崇拝に触れたことがなかった
She made him no definite answer
彼女は彼に明確な答えを与えなかった
but it was clear his words pleased her
しかし、彼の言葉が彼女を喜ばせているのは明らかだった
After that he talked to her whenever he could
その後、彼は可能な限り彼女に話しかけました
the valley became the world for him
渓谷は彼にとって世界となった
the world beyond the mountains seemed no more than

a fairy tale
山の向こうの世界はおとぎ話にしか見えなかった
perhaps one day he could tell her of these stories
いつの日か、彼は彼女にこれらの物語を話すことができるかもしれない
Very tentatively and timidly, he spoke to her of sight
非常に躊躇いがちに、そして臆病に、彼は彼女に視覚について語りかけた
sight seemed to her the most poetical of fancies
視覚は彼女にとって最も詩的な空想に思えた
she attentively listened to his description
彼女は注意深く彼の説明に耳を傾けた
he told her of the stars and the mountains
彼は彼女に星と山のことを話しました
and he praised her sweet white-lit beauty
そして、彼は彼女の甘い白く照らされた美しさを賞賛しました
She did not believe what he was saying
彼女は彼の言うことを信じなかった
and she could only half understand what he meant
そして、彼女は彼が何を言っているのか半分しか理解できませんでした
but she was mysteriously delighted
しかし、彼女は不思議なほど喜んでいました
and it seemed to him that she completely understood
そして、彼女が完全に理解しているように思えました
His love lost its awe and took courage
彼の愛は畏敬の念を失い、勇気を奪われました
He wanted to ask the elders for her hand in marriage
彼は長老たちに結婚の手を差し伸べてもらいたかったのです
but she became fearful and delayed
しかし、彼女は恐ろしくなり、遅れました
it was one of her elder sisters who first told Yacob
最初にヤコブに告げたのは姉の一人だった

she told him that Medina-sarote and Nunez were in love
彼女は彼に、メディナ・サローテとヌニェスが愛し合っていることを告げた
There was very great opposition to the marriage
結婚には大きな反対がありました
the objection wasn't because they valued her
反対は、彼女を大切にしているからではなかった
but they objected because they thought of him as different
しかし、彼らは彼を違うと思っていたので反対しました
he was still an idiot and incompetent thing for them
彼は彼らにとってまだ愚かで無能な存在でした
they classed him below the permissible level of a man
彼らは彼を人間の許容レベル以下に分類した
Her sisters opposed the marriage bitterly
彼女の姉妹は結婚に激しく反対した
they feared it would bring discredit on them all
彼らは、それが彼ら全員の信用を失墜させることを恐れた
old Yacob had formed a sort of liking for Nunez
年老いたヤコブはヌニェスに一種の好意を抱いていた
he was his nice, but clumsy and obedient serf
彼は彼の良い、しかし不器用で従順な農奴でした
but he shook his head at the proposal
しかし、彼はその提案に首を横に振った
and he said the thing could not be
そして、彼は事はあり得ないと言いました
The young men were all angry
若者たちは皆怒っていた
they did not like the idea of corrupting the race
彼らは、人種を堕落させるという考えを好まなかった
and one went so far as to strike Nunez
そして、一人はヌニェスを殴るところまで行った

but Nunez struck back at the man
しかし、ヌニェスは男に反撃した
Then, for the first time, he found an advantage in seeing
その時初めて、彼は見ることに利点を見いだした
even by twilight he could fight better than the blind man
黄昏時でさえ、彼は盲人よりもうまく戦うことができた
after that fight was over a new order had been established
その戦いが終わった後、新しい秩序が確立されました
no one ever thought of raising a hand against him again
誰も二度と彼に手を上げようとは思わなかった
but they still found his marriage impossible
しかし、彼らはまだ彼の結婚は不可能だと感じました
Old Yacob had a tenderness for his last little daughter
ヤコブ老人は、最後の幼い娘に優しさを抱いていた
he was grieved to have her weep upon his shoulder
彼は彼女が彼の肩で泣いていることを悲しんだ
"You see, my dear, he's an idiot"
「ほら、あいつは馬鹿だ」
"He has delusions about the world"
「彼は世界について妄想を抱いている」
"there isn't anything he can do right"
「彼にできることは何もない」
"I know," wept Medina-sarote
「わかってるわ」メディナ・サローテは涙を流した
"But he's better than he was"
「でも、あの時よりはマシになった」
"for all his trying he's getting better"
「努力の割には良くなっている」
"And he is strong and kind to me"
「そして、彼は私に強くて優しいです」

"stronger and kinder than any other man in the world"
「世界の誰よりも強くて優しい」

"And he loves me. And, father, I love him"
そして、彼は私を愛している。そして、お父さん、私は彼を愛しています」

Old Yacob was greatly distressed to find her inconsolable
ヤコブ老人は、彼女が慰められないのを見てひどく心を痛めました

what made it more distressing is he liked Nunez for many things
さらに悲惨なのは、彼がヌニェスを多くの点で気に入っていたことです

So he went and sat in the windowless council-chamber
それで、彼は行って、窓のない評議会の部屋に座りました

he watched the other elders and the trend of the talk
彼は他の長老たちと話の趨勢を観察した

at the proper time he raised his voice
適切なタイミングで彼は声を上げた

"He's better than he was when he came to us"
「彼は私たちのところに来たときよりも良くなっています」

"Very likely, some day, we shall find him as sane as ourselves"
「いつの日か、彼が私たちと同じように正気であることに気づくでしょう」

one of the elders thought deeply about the problem
長老の一人は、この問題について深く考えました

He was a great doctor among these people
彼はこれらの人々の中で偉大な医者でした

he had a very philosophical and inventive mind
彼は非常に哲学的で独創的な心を持っていました

the idea of curing Nunez of his peculiarities appealed

to him
ヌニェスの特異性を治すという考えは、彼にアピールした

another day Yacob was present at another meeting
別の日、ヤコブは別の会合に出席していた

the great doctor returned to the topic of Nunez
偉大な医者はヌニェスの話題に戻った

"I have examined Nunez," he said
「私はヌニェスを調べた」と彼は言った

"and the case is clearer to me"
「そして、この事件は私にはより明確です」

"I think very probably he might be cured"
「たぶん治るんじゃないかな」

"This is what I have always hoped," said old Yacob
「これは私がずっと望んでいたことだ」とヤコブ老人は言った

"His brain is affected," said the blind doctor
「彼の脳は影響を受けています」と盲目の医者は言った

The elders murmured in agreement
長老たちは同意して呟いた

"Now, what affects it?" asked the doctor
「さて、何が影響するのですか?」と医者は尋ねた

"This," said the doctor, answering his own question
「これだ」と医者は自分の質問に答えた

"Those queer things that are called the eyes"
「目と呼ばれる奇妙なもの」

"they exist to make an agreeable indentation in the face"
「彼らは顔に心地よいくぼみを作るために存在します」

"the eyes are diseased, in the case of Nunez"
「ヌニェスの場合、目は病気です」

"in such a way that it affects his brain"
「それが彼の脳に影響を与えるような方法で」

"his eyes bulge out of his face"

「彼の目は顔から膨らんでいる」
"he has eyelashes, and his eyelids move"
「睫毛が生えていて、まぶたが動く」
"consequently, his brain is in a state of constant irritation"
「その結果、彼の脳は常に刺激的な状態にあります」
"and so, everything is a distraction to him"
「だから、彼にとっては全てが気晴らしなのよ」
Yacob listened intently at what the doctor was saying
ヤコブは医師の言葉に熱心に耳を傾けた
"I think I may say with reasonable certainty that there is a cure"
「治療法はあると、それなりの確信を持って言えると思います」
"all we need to do is a simple and easy surgical operation"
「私たちがする必要があるのは、シンプルで簡単な外科手術だけです」
"all this involves is removing the irritant eyes"
「刺激の強い目を取り除くだけです」
"And then he will be sane?"
「そうすれば、彼は正気になるのだろうか?」
"Then he will be perfectly sane"
「そうすれば、彼は完全に正気になるだろう」
"and he'll be a quite admirable citizen"
「そして、彼は非常に立派な市民になるだろう」
"Thank Heaven for science!" said old Yacob
「科学を天に感謝します!」とヤコブ老人は言いました
and he went forth at once to tell Nunez of the good news
そして、すぐにヌニェスに朗報を伝えに行った
But Nunez wasn't quite as enthusiastic about the idea
しかし、ヌニェスはこのアイデアにそれほど乗り気ではなかった

he received the news with coldness and disappointment
彼は冷たさと失望をもってその知らせを受け取った
"the tone of your voice does not inspire confidence"
「声のトーンが自信を持てない」
"one might think you do not care for my daughter"
「あなたは私の娘を大事にしていないと思うかもしれません」
It was Medina who persuaded Nunez to face the blind surgeons
ヌニェスに盲目の外科医に立ち向かうよう説得したのはメディナだった
"You do not want me," he said, "to lose my gift of sight?"
「お前は俺に視力の賜物を失ってほしくないのか?」
She shook her head
彼女はかぶりを振った
"My world is sight"
「私の世界は視覚です」
Her head drooped lower
彼女の頭は低く垂れ下がった
"There are the beautiful things"
「美しいものがある」
"the world is full of beautiful little things"
「世界は美しい小さなものでいっぱいです」
"the flowers and the lichens amidst the rocks"
「岩の中の花と地衣類」
"the light and softness on a piece of fur"
「一切れの毛皮の軽さと柔らかさ」
"the far sky with its drifting dawn of clouds"
「雲の夜明けが漂う遥か空」
"the sunsets and the stars"
「夕焼けと星」
"And there is you"

「そして、君がいる」
"For you alone it is good to have sight"
「あなただけにとって、視力があるのは良いことです」
"to see your sweet, serene face sight is good"
「あなたの甘くて穏やかな顔を見るのは良いことです」
"to see your kindly lips"
「あなたの優しい唇を見るために」
"your dear, beautiful hands folded together"
「あなたの愛する美しい手を一緒に組んだ」
"it is these eyes of mine you won"
「お前が勝ったのは俺のこの目だ」
"it is these eyes that hold me to you"
「この瞳が私をあなたに抱きついている」
"but it is these eyes that those idiots seek"
「だが、あの馬鹿どもが求めているのは、この目だ」
"Instead, I must touch you"
「その代わり、私はあなたに触れなければなりません」
"I would hear you, but never see you again"
「君の声は聞こえるが、二度と会うことはない」
"must I come under that roof of rock and stone and darkness?"
「あの岩と石と暗闇の屋根の下に来なければならないのか?」
"that horrible roof under which your imaginations stoop"
「想像力をかきたてるあの恐ろしい屋根」
"no; you would not have me do that?"
「いや。私にそんなことをさせないの?」
A disagreeable doubt had arisen in him
不愉快な疑念が彼に生じた
He stopped and left the thing in question
彼は立ち止まり、問題のものを残しました
she said, "I wish sometimes you would not talk like that"

「たまにはそんな風に話さないでくれればいいのに」と。

"talk like what?" asked Nunez
「どんな話をするんだ?」ヌニェスが尋ねた

"I know your sight is pretty"
「君の視力が綺麗なのは知ってるよ」

"It is your imagination"
「それはあなたの想像力です」

"I love it, but now..."
「好きだけど、今は...」

He felt cold at the gravity of her words
彼は彼女の言葉の重大さに寒気を感じた

"Now?" he said, faintly
「今?」彼はかすかに言った

She sat quite still without saying anything
彼女は何も言わずにじっと座っていた

"you think, I would be better without my eyes?"
「目がない方がいいと思う?」

He was realising things very swiftly
彼は物事を非常に迅速に認識していました

He felt anger at the dull course of fate
彼は退屈な運命の経過に怒りを感じた

but he also felt sympathy for her lack of understanding
しかし、彼はまた、彼女の理解力のなさに同情した

but his sympathy for her was akin to pity
しかし、彼女に対する彼の同情は哀れみに似ていた

"Dear," he said to his love
「親愛なる」と彼は愛に言った

her spirit pressed against the things she could not say
言えないことに精神が押し寄せた

He put his arms about her and he kissed her ear
彼は彼女に腕を回し、彼女の耳にキスをした

and they sat for a time in silence
そして、二人はしばらく黙って座っていた

"If I were to consent to this?" he said at last
「もし私がこれに同意するなら?」彼はついに言った
in a voice that was very gentle
とても優しい声で
She flung her arms about him, weeping wildly
彼女は両腕で彼を抱きしめ、激しく泣いた
"Oh, if you would do that," she sobbed
「ああ、そんなことしてくれるなら」彼女はすすり泣いた
"if only you would do that one thing!"
「あんたがたった一つのことをしてくれたらいいのに!」
Nunez knew nothing of sleep in the week before the operation
ヌニェスは手術前の1週間、睡眠について何も知らなかった
the operation that was to raise him from his servitude and inferiority
彼を隷属と劣等感から引き上げるための作戦
the operation that was to raise him to the level of a blind citizen
彼を盲目の市民のレベルに引き上げる手術
while the others slumbered happily, he sat brooding
他の者たちが幸せそうに眠っている間、彼は憂鬱に座っていた
all through the warm, sunlit hours he wandered aimlessly
暖かく、太陽に照らされた時間の間中、彼はあてもなくさまよった
and he tried to bring his mind to bear on his dilemma
そして、彼は自分のジレンマに心を向けようとしました
He had given his answer and his consent
彼は答えと同意を与えた
and still he was not sure if it was right

それでも、それが正しいのかどうか確信が持てなかった
the sun rose in splendour over the golden crests
太陽は黄金の紋章の向こうに輝いて昇った
his last day of vision had began for him
彼の最後の幻視の日が始まった
He had a few minutes with Medina-sarote before she went to sleep
彼はメディナ・サローテが眠りにつくまで、数分間一緒に過ごした
"Tomorrow," he said, "I shall see no more"
「明日は」と彼は言った、「もう会えない」
"Dear heart!" she answered
「親愛なる心よ!」と彼女は答えた
and she pressed his hands with all her strength
そして彼女は全力で彼の手を押さえた
"They will hurt you, but little"
「彼らはあなたを傷つけるでしょうが、ほとんどありません」
"you are going to get through this pain"
「あなたはこの苦しみを乗り越えるつもりです」
"you are going through it, dear lover, for me"
「あなたはそれを経験しています、親愛なる恋人、私のために」
"if a woman's heart and life can do it, I will repay you"
「女の心と命がそれを成し遂げられるなら、私はあなたに報いる」
"My dearest one," she said in a tender voice, "I will repay"
「私の最愛の人」と彼女は優しい声で言った、「私は返済します」
He was drenched in pity for himself and her
彼は自分と彼女への哀れみに浸っていた
He held her in his arms and pressed his lips to hers
彼は彼女を腕に抱きしめ、唇を彼女の唇に押し付けた

and he admired her sweet face for the last time
そして、彼は最後に彼女の甘い顔を賞賛しました
"Good-bye!" he whispered to the dear sight of her
「さようなら!」彼は彼女の愛しい姿にささやいた
And then in silence he turned away from her
そして黙って、彼は彼女から顔を背けた
She could hear his slow retreating footsteps
ゆっくりと後退する彼の足音が聞こえた
something in the rhythm of his footsteps threw her into a passion of weeping
彼の足音のリズムに乗った何かが、彼女を泣き叫ぶ情熱へと駆り立てた
He had fully meant to go to a lonely place
彼は完全に孤独な場所に行くつもりだった
to the meadows with the beautiful white narcissus
綺麗な白水仙のいる牧草地へ
there he wanted remain until the hour of his sacrifice
彼は生贄の時までそこに留まりたかった
but as he walked he lifted up his eyes
しかし、歩きながら彼は目を上げた
and he saw the morning with his sight
そして、彼はその視力で朝を見た
it was like an angel shining in golden armour
それは黄金の鎧に輝く天使のようでした
he truly did love Medina-sarote
彼は本当にメディナ・サローテを愛していた
he was prepared to give up his sight for her
彼は彼女のために視力を捨てる覚悟をしていた
he was going to live the rest of his life in the valley
彼は残りの人生を渓谷で過ごすつもりだった
the angel marched down the steeps of the meadows
天使は牧草地の急斜面を行進した
and it bathed everything in its golden light
そして、それはすべてをその黄金の光で満たしました

without any notice something in him changed
何の予告もなく、彼の中の何かが変わった
the country of the blind was no more than a pit of sin
盲人の国は罪の穴にすぎなかった
He did not turn aside as he had meant to do
彼は、自分が意図したように、脇を向かなかった
but he went on and passed through the wall
しかし、彼は進み、壁を通り抜けました
from there he went out upon the rocks
そこから岩の上に出て行きました
his eyes were upon the sunlit ice and snow
彼の目は太陽に照らされた氷と雪に向けられていた
he saw their infinite beauty
彼は彼らの無限の美しさを見た
his imagination soared over the peaks
彼の想像力は峰々を飛び越えた
his thoughts went to the world he wouldn't see again
彼の思考は、二度と見ることのない世界へと向かった
he thought of that great free world
彼はその偉大な自由世界を思い浮かべた
the world that he was prepared to part from
彼が別れを覚悟した世界
the world that was his own
彼自身の世界
and he had a vision of those further slopes
そして、彼はそのさらなる斜面のビジョンを持っていた
his mind took him through the valleys he had come from
彼の心は、彼が来た谷を通り抜けた
he went along the river into the city
彼は川沿いに町に入った
in his mind he could see Bogota
彼の心の中にはボゴタが見えた
his imagination carried him through the city

彼の想像力は彼を街中へと運びました
a place of multitudinous stirring beauty
多彩で攪拌される美しさの場所
a glory by day, a luminous mystery by night
昼は栄光、夜は光り輝く神秘
a place of palaces and fountains
宮殿と噴水の場所
a place of statues and white houses
彫像と白い家の場所
his mind went with him out the city
彼の心は彼と共に街の外に行った
he followed the journey of a river
彼は川の旅をたどった
the river went through the villages and forests
川は村や森を通り抜けていました
a big steamer came splashing by
大きな汽船が水しぶきを上げて通り過ぎてきた
the banks of the river opened up into the sea
川の土手は海に開いていました
the limitless sea with its thousands of islands
何千もの島々が浮かぶ無限の海
he could see the lights of the islands and the ships
島々や船の明かりが見えた
life continued on each little island
それぞれの小さな島での生活は続いた
and he thought about that greater world
そして、彼はそのより大きな世界について考えました
he looked up and saw the infinite sky
見上げると、無限の空が見えた
it was not like the sky in the valley of the blind
それは盲人の谷の空のようではなかった
a small disk cut off by mountains
山々に遮られた小さな円盤
but, an arch of immeasurably deep blue

しかし、計り知れないほど深い青のアーチ
and in this he saw the circling of the stars
そして、この中に星々が回っているのが見えた

His eyes began to scrutinise the circle of mountains
彼の目は山々の輪を吟味し始めた

he looked at it a little keener than he had before
彼は以前よりも少し鋭くそれを見つめた

"perhaps one could go up that gully"
「あの峡谷に行けるかも」

"from there one could get to that peak"
「そこからあの山頂にたどり着ける」

"then one might come out among those pine trees"
「そうすれば、あの松の木の間から出てくるかもしれない」

"the slope past the pines might not be so steep"
「松林を過ぎた斜面はそんなに急ではないかも」

"and then perhaps that wallface can be climbed"
「そうすれば、あの壁面を登れるかもしれない」

"where the snow starts there will be a river"
「雪が降るところには川がある」

"from there there should be a path"
「そこから道があるはずだ」

"and if that route fails, to the East are other gaps"
「そして、そのルートが失敗すれば、東側には別のギャップがある」

"one would just need a little good fortune"
「ちょっとした幸運が必要だ」

He glanced back at the village
彼はちらりと村を振り返った

but he had to look at it once more
しかし、彼はもう一度それを見なければなりませんでした

he looked down into the country of the blind
彼は盲人の国を見下ろした

he thought of Medina-sarote, asleep in her hut
彼は小屋で眠っているメディナ・サローテのことを思い浮かべた
but she had become small and remote to him
しかし、彼女は彼にとって小さく、遠い存在になっていた
he turned again towards the mountain wall
彼は再び山の壁の方を向いた
the wall down which he had come down that day
あの日、彼が降りてきた壁を
then, very circumspectly, he began his climb
そして、非常に慎重な態度で、彼は登り始めた
When sunset came he was no longer climbing
日が暮れると、彼はもう登っていなかった
but he was far and high up the valley
しかし、彼は谷のはるか高いところにいました
His clothes were torn and his limbs were bloodstained
服は破れ、手足は血まみれだった
he was bruised in many places
彼はあちこちに打撲傷を負っていた
but he lay as if he were at his ease
しかし、彼はまるでくつろいでいるかのように横たわっていた
and there was a smile on his face
そして、彼の顔には笑みが浮かんでいた
From where he rested the valley seemed as if it were in a pit
彼が休んでいる場所からは、谷が穴の中にいるように見えました
now it was nearly a mile below him
今やそれは彼の1マイル近く下にあった
the pit was already dim with haze and shadow
穴は既に靄と影で薄暗くなっていた
the mountain summits around him were things of light

and fire
彼の周りの山頂は光と炎のものだった
the little things in the rocks were drenched with light and beauty
岩の中の小さなものは、光と美しさに満ちていました
a vein of green mineral piercing the grey
灰色を貫く緑色の鉱物の鉱脈
a flash of small crystal here and there
あちこちで小さなクリスタルの閃光
a minutely-beautiful orange light close to his face
微細なオレンジ色の光が顔に寄り添う
There were deep, mysterious shadows in the gorge
峡谷には深く神秘的な影があった
blue deepened into purple, and purple into a luminous darkness
青は紫に、紫は明るい闇に深まりました
over him was the endless vastness of the sky
彼の頭上には果てしなく広大な空が広がっていた
but he heeded these things no longer
しかし、かれは、もはやこれらのことに注意を払わなかった
instead, he laid very still there
それどころか、彼はそこにじっと横たわっていた
smiling, as if he were content now
まるで今、満足しているかのように微笑んでいる
content to have escaped from the valley of the Blind
盲人の谷から脱出した内容
the valley in which he had thought to be King
彼が王になると思っていた谷
the glow of the sunset passed
夕焼けの輝きが過ぎ去った
and the night came with its darkness
そして夜は暗闇とともにやってきた
and he lay there, under the cold, clear stars

そして、冷たく澄み切った星空の下に横たわっていた

The End
最後です

www.ingramcontent.com/pod-product-compliance
Lightning Source LLC
Chambersburg PA
CBHW012006090526
44590CB00026B/3904